Peter Munk Christiansen

Consensual Policy-Making

in the Nordic World

Aarhus University Press / The University of Wisconsin Press

The Nordic World
Consensual Policy-Making in the Nordic World

Cover, layout, and typesetting:
Camilla Jørgensen, Trefold
Cover photograph: Lars Kruse, AU
Copy editors: Heidi Flegal and Mia Gaudern
Acquisitions editors: Amber Rose Cederström
and Karina Bell Ottosen
This book is typeset in FS Ostro and printed
on Munken Lynx 130 g
Printed by Narayana Press, Denmark
Printed in Denmark 2024

ISBN 978 87 7597 004 9
ISBN 978 0 299 34374 3

This book is available in a digital edition

Library of Congress Cataloging-in-Publication
data is available

Published with the generous support of
the Aarhus University Research Foundation,
the Nordic Council of Ministers, and the
Danish Arts Foundation

The Nordic World series is copublished by
Aarhus University Press and the University
of Wisconsin Press

Aarhus University Press
aarhusuniversitypress.dk

The University of Wisconsin Press
uwpress.wisc.edu

Contents

Chapter 1.
Introduction 7

Chapter 2.
Mobilizing from the bottom up 13

Chapter 3.
The rise and reign of Nordic corporatism 27

Chapter 4.
Privileged pluralism 45

Chapter 5.
The Nordic labor market model 55

Chapter 6.
Voters, political parties, and parliamentary consensus-building 71

Chapter 7.
Reforming between consensus and conflict 87

Chapter 8.
Conclusions 103

Chapter 1.
Introduction

Compared to most other countries in the world, the Nordics stand out in a number of areas. By way of example, they all rank high on standard of living (Andersen 2021), equality (Jensen 2021), happiness (Bjørnskov 2021), and trust (Knutsen 2017). The Nordic countries are also distinct in the way they practice consensual conflict resolution, witnessed most clearly in their integration of special interest groups in public policymaking, in their labor market model, and in the consensus-seeking ways their parliaments work.

Every form of human society implies conflicts and questions about how to handle human interaction. Where are the limits between the rights and duties of the individual, the family, and society? How are power, wealth, and territory distributed among individuals and groups? Who can sanction, and how, if individuals or groups do not comply with norms or rules? How should healthcare be addressed, and how should education be organized and financed? Who should take care of preschool children, and how? The list goes on. Any modern society must make a multitude of decisions that will have consequences for most or many of the people in it – in one way or another.

In a democracy, these and many other questions are addressed and solved peacefully, without resorting to violence. Democracy is, in essence, peaceful conflict resolution.[1] In pre-democratic societies, the king or another sovereign might unanimously decide how to resolve a conflict, even if this involved the use of physical force. In a democracy, the army, the police, and the probation authorities are all under democratic political control. Democracy is the only system of governance which in principle gives all opportunities to take part in collective decision-making with consequences for their entire society, and to do so in a peaceful way.

1. An exception is the sanctioned use of physical violence. According to Max Weber (1919), the modern state holds a legitimate monopoly on using physical force. In a democracy, this monopoly is politically controlled

However, democracy is spelled out very differently in different countries. In his seminal book *Patterns of Democracy*, the Dutch-American political scientist Arend Lijphart (1999) distinguished between two ideal models of democracy: *majoritarian* and *consensual*. They were ideal in that they were stylized regarding certain properties and types that do not exist in any pure empirical form.

Majoritarian democracies accept a majority as a sufficient condition for making a decision, while a consensual democracy sees a majority as a minimum condition and regards including as many sides as possible as the ideal. Each system displays a syndrome of properties.

Many majoritarian systems use first-past-the-post electoral systems. Consequently, they tend to be two-party systems, run by single-party majority cabinets, alongside a pluralist system of interest groups with free competition among groups. Prominent examples are the United States and the United Kingdom.

Consensual systems have a proportional electoral system that allows multiple parties to be included in parliament and consequently enables multi-party systems to work. Most cabinets are multi-party coalitions in which parties share power. Such countries often have minority governments that are forced to find parliamentary majorities by including opposition parties. Finally, consensual democracies have a system of interest groups oriented towards the coordination of economic and other issues. Prominent examples are the Nordic countries, the Netherlands, Germany, and Austria.

Using data from several countries, Lijphart shows that consensual democracies tend to increase voter turnout, women's political representation, and voters' satisfaction with democracy, and also to bring the positions of voters and decision-makers closer together, and reduce economic inequality. While most scholars recognize Lijphart's empirical clustering of institutional properties, some disagree with his assertion that consensual systems are also "kinder and more gentle" (Lijphart 1999).

This book does not make value judgements on the merits of consensual versus majoritarian political systems. Nor does it systematically compare consensual and majoritarian systems, though such comparisons are presented now and then. Nor does the book portray the Nordic societies as heaven on Earth. They are not. They too face more or less unresolved problems of different kinds. High public spending and correspondingly high taxes affect people in ways that sometimes lead to suboptimal behavior. Immigration in some respects challenges a consensual culture created in times when societies were more homogeneous. Social pathologies such as drug abuse, suicide, domestic violence, and economic poverty are also found in the Nordic region. However, if, along the way, the reader senses that this author prefers a consensual to a majoritarian society, that merely bears witness to the fact that we all make value judgements, even when we are unaware of it.

A few initial remarks about the conception of the Nordic countries are also in order. In toto, the Nordics comprise Denmark, Finland, Iceland, Norway, and Sweden, plus the semi-autonomous countries Greenland, the Faroe Islands, and the Åland Islands. The three Scandinavian countries – Denmark, Norway, and Sweden – are a sub-group of the Nordics, and they do not share, say, Finland's dramatic history of complicated relations with Russia, or Iceland's small population and outlying geographical location in the middle of the North Atlantic.

Admittedly, Denmark figures more prominently in this book than its actual fair share, its author being Danish, and Scandinavia figures more prominently than either Finland or Iceland. The latter two countries receive comparatively little attention in the analysis.

This book is intended to paint a portrait of a group of societies, particularly in Scandinavia, which share the practice of consensual conflict resolution by means of a wide range of political and other societal institutions. Several academic colleagues – Helene Helboe Pedersen, Christoffer Green-Pedersen, Carsten Jensen, and David Andersen – have provided helpful comments along the way, and so have the Danish editor, my language reviewer Annette Bruun Andersen, and the book's anonymous peer reviewer and publisher. They all deserve my thanks.

I will begin, in Chapter 2, by focusing on the societal prerequisites for the consensual systems in the Nordic countries. While consensual democracy as such was hardly ever planned, it is by no means accidental that the Nordics arrived at it. Early mobilization of peasants and later urban workers laid the groundwork for strong civil societies, a high level of equality, and strong unions. Major political and economic challenges, such as rapidly changing international developments and urbanization, were handled in ways that accommodated broad groups. Inclusion of civil society in policy formulation and implementation proved to create satisfactory solutions that enjoyed widespread legitimacy. Chapter 2 does not attempt to explain in great detail why consensual democracy came to prevail in Scandinavia, but rather seeks to follow some of the significant paths in this development.

Corporatism, the theme of Chapter 3, is not a Nordic invention. It has its roots in late nineteenth-century Catholic thinking and was associated with the Italian brand of fascism promoted by Benito Mussolini. Nevertheless, the Nordic countries adopted corporatism as a significant element in their governance structures, but without any links to fascist thinking. The Nordic countries are known to have comparatively strong corporatist structures, although with some differences. Corporatism – defined as the institutionalized integration of organized interests in policy-making and implementation – had its golden age in the three to four decades following World War II (1939–1945).

Chapter 4 is devoted to the period after the heyday of corporatism. During the 1970s and 1980s, economic restructuring and reforms reduced the value of corporatism as a means of structuring decision-making. New issues arose on the political agenda, and new types of interest groups and social movements came to play a more important role. Some of corporatism's characteristics became less pronounced, while others remained central to Nordic political and administrative decision-making. Binderkrantz, Christiansen, and Pedersen (2014) have suggested that "privileged pluralism" was and still is a characteristic of the shifting relations between central decision-makers and interest groups.

Chapter 5 discusses another common trait of the Nordic region: the labor market model. This model implies a high degree of labor market self-governance, where some matters regulated by the state are governed (in most of the countries) in collaboration between trade unions and employer organizations. This model presupposes strong labor market organizations, which many countries elsewhere do not have. The Nordic labor market model also presupposes close coordination between the state and the "social partners" (as the workers' unions and employer organizations on the two sides of the negotiating table are often called), and in this respect the model bears some resemblance to corporatism. The Nordic labor market model is, to some extent, a barrier against poor working conditions, the growth of a working precariat, and the decommodification of the labor force due to unemployment and sickness.

When the term *consensual decision-making* is used, most people instinctively think about decision-making processes in parliaments. Chapter 6 focuses precisely on the Nordic parliaments. Many decisions made by elected politicians in the Nordics are reached by oversized majorities, by coalitions of parties that are larger than is strictly necessary to make a decision. This is part of consensual decision-making. But why do governments pursue oversized majorities when they have an implicit policy cost for the government? This question is at the very core of Nordic parliamentary behavior. Oversized majorities follow from the logic of bloc politics. At the same time, oversized majorities signal consensus, and oversized legislation reduces uncertainty for citizens and businesses because it reduces the likelihood of legislative changes if the government changes color – noting that in Nordic political coloring, "blue" signifies conservative and fiscal-liberal parties while "red" signifies social-democratic and left-oriented parties.

Meanwhile, consensual policy-making can run into a potential stalemate problem. Change and reform will be limited to outcomes that are backed by all important actors. Radical change – or just change that severely contradicts the interests of strong groups in society – will be impossible or at best difficult. But what happens if a powerful actor – say, a government – has a strong preference for radical reform? Chapter 7 looks at the balance between the need for conflictual reform and Nordic consensual policy-making, before Chapter 8 wraps up with some conclusions.

Chapter 2.

Mobilizing from the bottom up

All countries are products of their history. History is created in the intersection of structures and preconditions on the one hand and human agency on the other. Human beings always have some degree of freedom, but they are also subject to natural, economic, social, and cultural constraints. Viewed from a distance, the Scandinavian countries share various traits that help explain the development of consensual democracies in the twentieth century. If we take a closer look, however, differences emerge – some quite significant – and indeed, any other observation would nullify the effects of human agency. Nevertheless, we do find interesting similarities in the journeys of all three Scandinavian countries from absolute monarchy towards consensual democracy.

These similarities include relatively peaceful and virtually bloodless transformations from absolute to constitutional monarchies, the mobilizing of peasants and workers in the late nineteenth century, and experiences with wars and economic crises in the first half of the twentieth century.

Bloodless bourgeois revolutions

One clue to the Scandinavian countries' evolution into consensual democracies is that their transitions from pre-democratic rule to the initial stage of democratic rule was more peaceful than in most other countries. Scandinavian democratization was, in fact, exceptionally peaceful, though it took various paths. Even so, there were certainly elements of conflict, and some bloodshed as well.

In Sweden, a bloodless coup d'état in 1809 led to a new constitution that same year. This ended the period of "enlightened royal absolutism" and created a constitutional monarchy that relied on the *Riksdag* assembly,[2] which comprised representative groups from the four so-called estates of society: the nobility, the church, the urban bourgeoisie, and the peasantry. This group representation arrangement was abolished in 1865 and replaced by two chambers in the Riksdag. Due, among other things, to its strict limitations on voting rights, Sweden could not reasonably be termed a democratic state based on its 1809 constitution or even its 1865 reform. Still, it says something about the country's peaceful and gradual path towards democracy that the 1809 constitution was only formally superseded by a new constitution in 1974 (Larsson 1993). It is customary among Swedish scholars to regard 1921, the year Swedish women got full suffrage rights, as the beginning of modern Swedish democracy (Wängnerud 2012). Sweden has adhered to parliamentarism since 1917.

2. The Riksdag – Sweden's now unicameral parliament – currently has 350 members who are elected every fourth year, although extraordinary elections can be held between two general elections

Norway took a very different path. For almost 300 years (1537-1814), Denmark and Norway formed a national alliance called a "personal union" with a succession of Danish kings as their joint ruler. When Denmark found itself on the losing side in the Napoleonic Wars, it was forced to relinquish Norway in 1814. But during a few weeks of April and May 1814, a group of Norwegian men – a group that in many ways represented Norwegian society, broadly speaking – wrote a new document, the Eidsvoll Constitution, that was an equivalent to the Swedish Constitution of 1809. However, while the Eidsvoll Constitution remained in force, the Norwegian quest for total independence was lost during a two-week war with Sweden in the summer of 1814. Norway did get its own parliament – the *Storting*[3] – but it once again ended up in a personal union arrangement, this time under Swedish rule. This union was dissolved in 1905 when Norway also became an independent state. Local government suffrage was adopted in Norway in 1910; universal voting rights at a national level came in 1913.

3. The Norwegian unicameral parliament – the Storting – currently has 169 members, who earn their seats in general elections held every four years

Denmark followed a third path. Absolute monarchy was not abolished until 1848. The Danish "revolution" took place in early 1848, under a king who was influenced by the revolts and threats of revolution he saw taking place in Germany and France around that time. On March 21, 1848, a procession of some 12,000 to 15,000 people marched through Copenhagen, demanding a new constitution. When the protestors arrived at the royal castle, King Frederik VII, who had been on the throne for just two months, announced that he was willing to step down as absolute monarch in favor of a constitutionally ruled kingdom. But before a new constitution was adopted in 1849, civil war broke out further afield: While the transition in the capital of Copenhagen was peaceful, the two southerly duchies of Schleswig and Holstein protested the king's decision, sparking a three-year civil war. The Danes won this war, but they ultimately lost both of the South Jutland duchies to Prussia in the war of 1864.

Although the new Danish constitution, adopted in 1849, was probably one of the most liberal in Europe at the time, it did not introduce democracy in Denmark. Voting rights to the parliament[4] were limited to "respectable" men who had their own household and were aged 30 or older. Around 15 percent of the population fulfilled those

4. The Danish unicameral parliament – the *Folketing* – currently has 179 members. General elections are held at four-year intervals, although a general election is often called before the four-year term has expired

requirements. Furthermore, the king appointed his governments without due respect for the composition of the more representative of the two chambers, the *Folketing*. Parliamentarism, which means ensuring that the government is appointed in accordance with the majority in parliament, was not installed in Denmark until 1901. Women's suffrage was introduced in 1907 for local elections and, with the 1915 constitution, for national elections too.

Mobilizing the peasantry

In addition to laying the constitutional foundation for Scandinavia's democracies, the nineteenth century delivered remarkable improvements for both peasants and workers. Two such movements particularly affected the growth of consensual Scandinavian politics and thus had profound consequences for present Scandinavian societies: the peasants' movement and the workers' movement.

The special interest organizations of rural groups in the Nordics have historically played an important role in the region's public policies, and the agrarian political parties – *Venstre* in Denmark (a pro-free market, right-centrist party whose name somewhat confusingly means "the left") and the Centre Parties in Norway and Sweden – remain important parliamentary players today (Widfeldt 2001). Nordic peasant history is long, but suffice it to say that in the pre-industrial Scandinavian economies, peasants and fishermen generated most of the nations' GDPs.

Life in medieval agrarian Scandinavian societies was hard, brutal, and brief. In fact, most of the common folk barely managed to survive. From the late eighteenth century, however, agricultural reforms and technical advances improved life somewhat, at least for those who owned their own farms. In Denmark, adscription[5] prevented peasants from leaving their farms; they were obliged to work for their local landlord in return for his protection. This practice, which was by no means a fair or balanced

5. A form of serfdom, in Danish called *stavnsbåndet* (loosely: "the bond to one's place of origin"), the statute of adscription meant that men aged 18 to 36 had to live where they were born. This statute gave landlords and the military control over the working capacity of the men adscribed to their area. https://www.familysearch.org/en/wiki/Denmark_Adscription_of_1733_(Stavnsb%C3%A5ndet)

exchange of goods or labor, was repealed in the late 1700s under the influences of European Enlightenment thinking. From that time on, peasants could gradually begin to develop their farms more independently.

Although sixteenth-century Norway was ruled by the Danish kings from Copenhagen, Norwegian peasants had more freedom than their Danish counterparts, probably because the estate of the nobility was smaller and weaker in the north. The Danish administration also introduced reforms that loosened the strictures binding Norwegian peasants, albeit with the purposes of improving state control over the recruitment of soldiers and building out the Norwegian tax base and the expansive, mountainous country's infrastructure in general.

In Sweden the peasants had some leverage through the stands, or estate-based assemblies – nobility, church, bourgeoisie, and the peasantry – which, as mentioned, survived absolutism. Essentially, the Swedish Riksdag was a large, national stand-type assembly until 1865.

In Denmark the stands were abolished under absolute rule, but they were re-established between 1834 and 1848, as a prelude to democracy. Although the peasantry was the weakest social estate of the four they could still raise issues and put demands on the political agenda.

The writer, thinker, and pastor N.F.S. Grundtvig published his first writings on what would later grow into the Danish folk high school movement during the 1830s. These pieces were based on Enlightenment ideas, combining the prevailing confidence in science and technical advancements on the one hand, and the ideal of educating "the people" to handle democracy on the other. The first Danish folk high school opened in 1844, and by 1872 there were 52 in all. Most of those attending the many live-in folk high school courses were young men from solid, farm-owning families. These future smallholders and farmers gained self-confidence, acquired new knowledge, and also learned useful professional and technical skills. Cathie Jo Martin (2018) finds that, in general – meaning beyond the agricultural instruction – teaching in the Nordic countries was, and is, about more than the actual skills students learn; it is also a process of cultural education, *Bildung* or formation, which aims to foster social inclusion, democratic norms, local community spirit, and a civic mindset.

The 1860s saw a gradual transformation in Denmark from grain to animal production, spurred by innovations such as butter centrifuge technology. In the late 1870s, Danish grain crops were priced out by cheap grain from overseas, which could be transported at low prices by the new sea-going steamships. Consequently, small farmers had to increase the added value of their products by intensifying animal production.

Instead of setting up privately owned for-profit firms, small Danish farmers began to take a collaborative approach that would soon grow into a huge cooperative movement. The country's folk high schools played a large role in this development, as they had given the rural population the skills and sufficient class consciousness to enable them to act for and by themselves. Thousands of cooperatives appeared, all across the country. Most were dairies, but there were also cooperative abattoirs, and coops set up to make collective purchases of grain, fertilizer, and other goods became a common sight. In addition, joint standards for product quality were introduced, meaning that farmers could sell commodities like Danish bacon, butter, and eggs that met high, uniform quality requirements.

The basic principles for these cooperative undertakings were: 1) democratic election of the management; 2) one vote for every member, regardless of the size of their farm; 3) investment of all profits in the cooperative, or the return of profits to members; and 4) collective liability of all members for the cooperative's debt. Scholars have also seen this as a critique of the growing trend towards industrial capitalism at the time: In the rural cooperative, a farmer's income was determined by the efforts of himself and his family, not by who owned the means of production (Gundelach 1988: 122).

Some Danish cooperatives are still alive and thriving today. Numerous mergers of small dairies have created Arla, one of the world's largest diary conglomerates, which is collectively owned by farmer-members in several countries, mainly Sweden and Denmark. Similarly, numerous cooperative slaughterhouses have gradually merged into Danish Crown, one of the world's ten largest meat-producing companies, and still owned by the farmer-members who breed and deliver the livestock.

As a superstructure for these many farmers and their cooperatives, Danish agriculture formed an influential set of interest groups to service their members, and to promote and guard their interests vis-à-vis the state. Danish agriculture became part of the corporatist system, a development discussed in Chapter 3.

Scandinavian peasants – and later farmers – made several contributions to consensual democracy. Among the most important were peaceful cooperation with the state during their disentanglement from the nobility; the focus on education and folk high schools; and the strong sense of civil coherence in rural communities that created strong and enduring cooperatives.

In short, Danish agriculture stepped into the twentieth century with self-confidence and pride, and with a set of strong collective organizations such as cooperatives, export companies, and special interest groups. Due to the agricultural sector's importance for the Danish economy, Danish farmers and their organizations were relatively stronger than their Nordic colleagues. For many across the region, farming was more difficult and less productive due to climatic and geographical circumstances. Nevertheless, farmers in Norway and Sweden also played an important role in the development of twentieth-century consensus democracy.

Finally, as already mentioned, rural populations in the Nordics added a political arm to their superstructure. All Scandinavian countries have had – and still have – agrarian parties with close ties to farmers' organizations. In 1870, the Danish agrarian party was established, followed by the Swedish and Norwegian agrarian parties in 1913 and 1920, respectively. They have all been important in political and parliamentarian terms, and they all survived the dramatic drop in the number of farmers after World War II, resulting from the adoption of new and far more productive agricultural techniques. Today, the formal ties between agrarian parties and the agricultural community have weakened or disappeared, but these parties still champion agricultural interests.

So why were the journeys of Scandinavia's peasant populations, from poverty and serfdom to a life as independent farmers, more peaceful and pervasive than in many other countries? David Andersen (2023a) shows that for the peasant classes, the early introduction of meritocratic bureaucracy and an impartial administration made a huge difference. France and Prussia, which shared some preconditions – for instance low agricultural productivity – with the Scandinavian countries, introduced impartial administration much later than the Scandinavian countries. There were several reasons for this, notably their involvement in various wars.

Meritocratic bureaucracy implies the abolition of patrimonialism and bribery. With meritocratic and impartial state administrations and state control over local administrations, the Scandinavian states were able to implement agricultural reforms in ways that implied more inclusive processes for formulating and implementing policies. This also dampened the distributive conflicts that implicitly follow reforms. Andersen (2023a) shows that despite country-based differences, there was less dissatisfaction and discontent among Scandinavian nobility and landowners who lost power and control due to the reforms than among their counterparts in countries like France, with its history of revolutions.

Meritocratic and impartial administration is a strong and important asset for any society, and not only in connection with agrarian reforms. Meritocratic administration reduces corruption, increases efficiency, and makes reforms more likely to succeed (Dahlström and Lapuente 2014). Consequently, the early introduction of impartial reform processes smoothed Scandinavia's way forward.

Mobilizing and unionizing urban workers

The working classes of the Nordic countries have been and remain more politically powerful than workers in most other countries – though they were inspired by trade unions in other European countries, particularly Germany. Nordic trade unions organize some 52 to 67 percent of wage-earners. Strong unions play a very special and independent role in Nordic labor market policies (as explained in Chapter 5), helping to balance the relationship between employers and employees. Likewise, the strong social-democratic parties in the Nordics grew from blue-collar ranks. This means that understanding present-day Scandinavian politics calls for some basic historical knowledge of the Nordic labor unions and their contributions to the cooperative society.

While the mobilization of the Nordic peasantry was a drawn-out affair, the Nordic working classes mobilized swiftly after the sudden wave of industrialization in the late nineteenth century created significant economic and social problems in the cities.

Scandinavia's first modern-style trade union, founded in 1848 in Norway, organized agricultural workers rather than urban industrial workers. The movement was suppressed, however, and its founder imprisoned, so it was not until 1872 that the first Norwegian urban trade union – organizing typographers – was established. In 1899 the first umbrella organization for all blue-collar unions was established. The Norwegian Trade Union Federation became, and remains, a major player in Norwegian society. The same goes for the Swedish and Danish trade union federations.

Typographers were also behind the first national trade union in Sweden, founded in 1886, and unionization was even more rapid here than in the other two countries. Estimates say that the Swedish unions had around 15,000 members in 1890; nearly 70,000 in 1900; and a total of 230,000 members in 1907. This should be compared to the approximately 388,000 people working in factories, in mines, and as skilled craftsmen around that time, which means that about 60 percent of potential members were paying their monthly membership fee (Blake 1960).

In Denmark, the first workers' associations were established in the 1850s, but it was not until the early 1870s that socialist ideology became associated with the trade union movement. Things also developed quickly in Denmark. The number of unions grew to 109 in 1890; 239 in 1896; and 302 in 1908 (Gundelach 1988: 143).

Importantly, with the advent of the socialist trade unions, political arms also began to develop, in the form of social-democratic parties. The Social Democratic Party in Denmark was established in 1871; its Norwegian counterpart in 1887; and their Swedish counterpart in 1889.

The pace of industrialization, the rapid growth of the labor unions, and the development of a new working-class party caused concern and anxiety among the property-owning classes. This is hardly surprising in light of the violent conflicts in many continental European countries, where demonstrations and strikes presaged imminent revolution. Predictably, the unions were counteracted by the bourgeoisie, who were sometimes aided by the police and armed forces. In 1871 a fight erupted in Copenhagen between workers on the one side and police and military on the other. This skirmish, called the Battle on the Common, resulted in several wounded workers, policemen, and soldiers, but without loss of life.[6]

6. The Battle on the Common was the first and only violent confrontation between authorities and workers during the birth of the Danish union movement

The unions soon grew too strong to be beaten back by the bourgeoisie. The saying "if you can't beat them, join them" is well illustrated by a Danish example. After a series of tough strikes and lockouts, the Danish Employers' Confederation and the Danish Confederation of Trade Unions hammered out an agreement called the September Compromise in 1899, which has since been referred to as the founding constitution of the Danish labor market. The gist of this agreement is that the trade unions recognize the employers' exclusive managerial right to hire and fire employees, while the employers recognize the workers' right to organize. Each side accepts the other's right to take action (to lock out employees or strike, respectively) if a collective agreement cannot be reached amicably (Due, Madsen, & Jensen 2000). These basic principles still apply today in different guises in the Scandinavian countries, for instance when regular collective agreements on salary and working conditions are being negotiated, which routinely takes place every few years. On rare occasions a strike will follow a "nay" vote if an agreement cannot gain enough support from union members.

The institutionalization of the Nordic workers' movement was not limited to work-related issues and the political issues cleared with the social-democratic parties. The national movements came to control networks with many types of organizations relevant to their members' societal, cultural, social, educational, and private lives. Socialist newspapers, reading and discussion clubs, sports clubs, amateur theaters, workers' cooperatives, publishers, and concerts are examples that show how widely the movements influenced the newly mobilized working class.

World War I (1914-1918) and the Bolshevik Revolution in 1917 created splits in the Scandinavian unions and social-democratic parties. The communists broke away from the Socials Democrats in Denmark and Sweden, and a new Communist Party was created in Norway in 1923. The social-democratic parties saw peaceful, democratic reforms as the way forward, and cooperating with employers and the bourgeoisie was part of their ongoing struggle for bettering working-class lives.

The strong Nordic trade unions were born out of conflict, not consensus. Even so, they greatly contributed to the development of consensual labor market relations and consensual democracy during the twentieth century by establishing different institutional conflict-resolution measures. To some extent, the organizational and political strength of the trade unions helped to counter the political influence of businesses, trade, and industry.

The Lutheran state churches

In Sweden, Denmark, and Norway, the Lutheran reformation took place in the 1520s and 1530s. The independent political role of the Catholic Church was eliminated when its lands and assets were transferred to the Crown in Sweden and in the Dano-Norwegian kingdom, with the sovereigns also becoming the heads of the Church in their own countries. This also meant that the Church's role in social welfare was transferred to the state (Koefoed 2017). Lutheranism has thus been seen as the antecedent of the Scandinavian universal welfare states, and scholars have discussed whether Lutheranism laid the foundation for Nordic consensual democracy. However, David Andersen (2023b) points to the fact that Prussia was also a Lutheran state until its unification with the other German states in 1871, but Prussia did not develop along the same consensual path as the Scandinavian countries; nor did the German welfare state (Esping-Andersen 1990). There may be some relationship between Lutheranism and consensual democracy, but if there is, it cannot be simple.

Strong Nordic civil societies

Alexis de Tocqueville (2004/1835) noted in his famous book *Democracy in America* that civil societies play an important role as an intermediate organizational layer between the state and its citizens. According to another French political philosopher, Charles-Louis de Secondat Montesquieu, civil societies induce citizens to handle their own affairs without state interference. When people solve shared problems in groups and organizations that they control, they also create cooperative relationships among themselves. Civil societies have played, and still play, an important role in creating the contemporary Nordic countries. Other strong civil society groups besides agrarian organizations and trade unions have been, and remain, active in economic matters (such as credit associations, cooperatives, and housing associations) and in the fields of sports, leisure activities, identity, and religion.

Strong civil societies are not a sufficient condition for consensual societies, however. Alexis de Tocqueville (2004/1835) noted that America – by which he meant the United States of America – had a very strong civil society. That may still be true in many areas, but it has certainly not helped the US pursue a path of consensual policy-making. On the contrary. And it is worth noting that a precondition for the peaceful transformation of Scandinavian agriculture in the eighteenth and early nineteenth centuries was the introduction of impartial administration practices. There is nevertheless good reason to believe that the strong civil structures in the Nordic countries have played a part in the development and the preservation of the region's consensual societies.

Chapter 3.

The rise and reign of Nordic corporatism

Corporatism is a contested concept and phenomenon. In a Scandinavian context, it is mostly understood as the "institutionalized and privileged integration of organized interests in the preparation and/or implementation of public policies" (Christiansen et al. 2010: 27). The core of corporatism is that involving politically important interest groups in forming and implementing policies ensures that the resulting policies respect the groups and also comply with a preference for consensual policy-making. *Institutionalized* in this context implies a repeated and regularized relationship; and *privileged* means that not all special interest groups have the same weight in the relationship (Christiansen et al. 2010). Some groups earn their status as privileged – that is, recognized by the state as representing a larger group – by complying with the norms and standards of corporatism. Privileged partners get concessions in return for accepting, supporting, and complying with the outcome of negotiations. However, sometimes they too must face defeat. In the latter case, access to decision-making arenas probably reduces the loss, compared to a situation in which an interest group is completely left out of the process (Öberg et al. 2011).

Corporatism as a concept comes with a burden: It has its origin in nineteenth-century Catholic thinking, but was later adopted by fascist thinkers. The idea was that parliaments were not supposed to reflect political parties on the right and left but were to reflect society's different "corporations" – employers, workers, farmers, craftsmen, and so on. These were a parallel to the pre-democratic stands that assembled representatives from the four estates: the nobility, the church, the peasantry, and the bourgeoisie (Christiansen 2019). Benito Mussolini actually instituted a corporatist governance structure in Fascist Italy, which was in force from the 1920s into the 1940s.

Today's corporatism has nothing in common with fascist thinking. Modern corporatism is neither a political ideology nor a philosophy, but a way of preparing and implementing political and administrative decisions.

Political give and take

Corporatism can be portrayed as a kind of political give and take, as indicated in Figure 3.1. Special interest groups are allowed to influence the political agenda and political and administrative decisions, in return for sharing two of their assets with politicians and civil servants. The first is information, which is needed to make decisions more targeted, effective, and efficient. Interest groups know their members and are, in many cases, close to the economic and social reality that civil servants and politicians wish to affect. Such information is valuable to decision-makers who want to maximize policy gains but have little knowledge about the object they want to regulate. This is a technical-instrumental role of interest groups.

The second asset – which is just as important as the first – is the political support that interest groups can give.

Figure 3.1 A model of the give-and-take relationship between decision-makers and interest groups

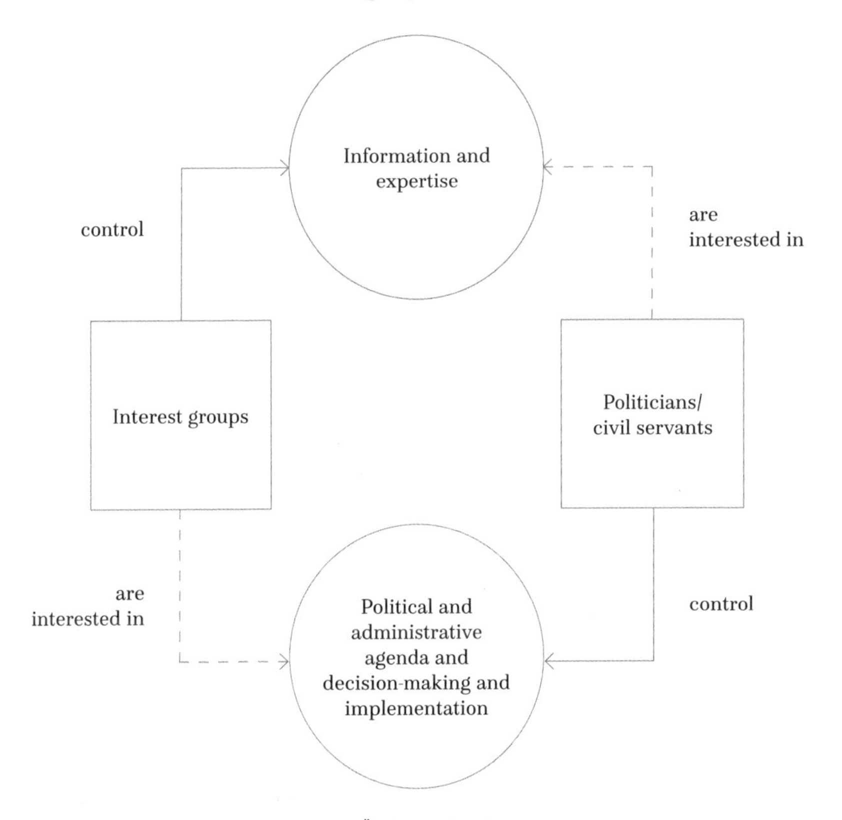

Source: Developed from Öberg et al. (2011)

Governments need support for policies they are considering, and currently pursuing, and they hope to do better in parliament and among the electorate by virtue of endorsements from interest groups. An endorsement or the absence of criticism from strong interest groups makes the government's decisions appear better to the opposition, the media, and the electorate. The explicit consent of interest groups is also believed to enhance successful policy implementation, meaning the life a given law has after it is enacted by parliament.

Allow me to illustrate: Danish evidence shows that center-right governments can increase the propensity of the social-democratic party to vote in favor of the government's labor market proposals if they originate from commission work that includes union representatives. The logic is that it is hard for the Social Democrats to criticize a proposal that has been endorsed by union representatives. Conversely, it has been shown that social-democratic governments can increase the agrarian/fiscal-liberal party *Venstre*'s propensity to vote in favor of agricultural legislation that originates from commission work in which agrarian interest groups have been involved. Again, it is difficult for a traditionally close political ally of agriculture to oppose proposals endorsed by agricultural groups. Thus, corporatism creates parliamentary consensus (Christiansen & Nørgaard 2003).

The logic behind political give and take is applied in most liberal democracies, as it is often viewed as beneficial for both interest groups and political decision-makers. In the Nordic countries it has conquered many – perhaps even most – policy sectors as such exchanges gradually became more deeply entrenched, and relations between interest groups and decision-makers grew closer than in most other countries; the UK and the US are examples of the opposite arrangement.

Early corporatism

Scandinavian corporatism is not the result of some grand design. Its original actors were strong civil societies with well-organized farmers, workers, employers, and industrialists on one side, all in pursuit of politically favorable decisions; and political and administrative decision-makers on the other, in pursuit of solutions to societal problems. Its processes were cooperative trials and errors, along with some imports from abroad, in the quest for feasible and acceptable solutions to societal problems both large and small (Christiansen & Nørgaard 2003).

In Denmark it became common for certain newly established special interest groups to contact parliamentarians as early as the 1880s. However, corporatist structures involving the agrarian organizations did not form until after the turn of the century. While the farmers' interest groups grew strong during the 1870s (see Chapter 2), they did not seek state assistance to reorient their production towards raising livestock. They became corporatist partners quite late, but from the early 1930s through the late 1960s corporatist ties were very strong between agriculture and the Danish state. In some cases agricultural organizations administered state-financed programs without any national authorities interfering on the operative side. Such arrangements became known as *private-interest government*. With Denmark's entry into the EEC[7] in 1973, this arrangement between the state and the farmers' organizations was no longer workable.

7. Denmark became a member of the European Economic Community on January 1, 1973. In 1993 the EEC was transformed into the European Union (EU), as a sign of even deeper integration

It was the urban bourgeoisie's concerns about the so-called *worker's question* that spurred the first corporatist encounters: What to do about all the problems caused by rapid urbanization and industrialization – social unrest and economic imbalances, inadequate infrastructure, housing, and public health, and poverty? In Denmark, a Workers' Commission, established in 1875, dealt with various issues related to social security, but workers were not directly represented in this commission. The first corporatist commission with workers' representation – signaling the rapidly growing trade union movement – was the Workers' Insurance Commission, established in the early twentieth century, which addressed insurance for workers injured on the job. This was followed by a permanent forum, the Workers' Council, which had different tasks related to working environment issues (Nørgaard 1997). The first institutional manifestation of corporatism in Denmark is therefore linked to the labor market. But corporatism was not a social-democratic invention in Scandinavia: Corporatist structures were born long before the Social Democrats became the strongest political party.

Generally speaking, this pattern also characterized early Swedish and Norwegian corporatism. Particularly in Sweden, the trade unions were very strong (Rothstein 1992; Lewin 1994; Svensson 2013). In 1907 they had significantly more members than the Danish and Norwegian unions combined, and were seen as a threat to the existing political and social order. As it turned out, policies negotiated between state actors and representatives for the employers and workers actually dampened social conflicts.

The Ghent system

One way of administrating unemployment benefits is known as the *Ghent system*. When benefits are subsidized by the state, topping up members' own contributions, the defining aspect of this system is that the money is administered by private organizations – unemployment insurance funds – with close ties to the trade unions (Scruggs 2002). It therefore gives unions some control over the administration of unemployment benefits. The Ghent system, named after the Belgian city where it was first implemented, was introduced in many countries in the early nineteenth century, and it came to play an important role for more than a hundred years, particularly in Denmark and Sweden. Among the Nordic countries, Denmark was first to introduce it (in 1907), followed by Norway (in 1915), Finland (in 1917), Sweden (in 1934), and Iceland (in 1955).

In the case of Denmark, the Ghent system was a compromise between the agrarian/fiscal-liberal party *Venstre* and the urban Conservative Party: Introducing state subsidies could ease the social unrest related to unemployment. Running a voluntary system outside the state apparatus also kept the countryside, where unionization was low, out of the system. Finally, administrative costs could be kept down by embedding the benefit system in a non-state-run setting.

Most countries later abolished the Ghent system, many in favor of a mandatory, tax-financed system. Interestingly, the countries that have kept the Ghent system – Denmark, Sweden, Finland, Iceland, and to some extent Belgium – have significantly higher unionization rates than those which abolished it (see Table 3.1). Two countries call for special mention: Belgium has comparatively high union density but no longer a full Ghent system. Norway has relatively high union density, but it is clearly lower than in the other Nordic countries, having abandoned the Ghent system in 1938. As the only Nordic country to make this decision, it even did so under a Labor government. The Norwegian government for some reason preferred a state-run system to the union-run Ghent system (Kjellberg & Neergaard 2022).

The correlation between a country's use of the Ghent system and its union density is believed to be causal. It rests on the close relationship between the administrators of unemployment benefits and the trade unions (Scruggs 2002). In a way, the correlation is the result of an illusion among employees that unemployment insurance is contingent on union membership. In many cases, however, it is not. Nevertheless, maintaining the Ghent system has been a battle between center-left and center-right political parties, with the latter trying to undermine the strong positions of the trade unions (Klitgaard & Nørgaard 2014). It is one of political history's great ironies that measures to combat unemployment and keep public expenditure down, which were introduced by the center-right parties in the early twentieth century, went on to become one of the strongest footholds of the Nordic labor unions.

The reason the Ghent system deserves so much attention is that high union density has massive consequen-

Table 3.1 The introduction and later status of the Ghent system in the Nordics and selected other European countries, alongside unionization rates

The Ghent system			Unionization rate		
	Introduction	**Abolition**	**1960**	**2000**	**2019 (or most recent prior to 2019)**
Belgium	1901 (Ghent)/1920	Still operating	41.5	56.6	49.1
France	1905	1950	20.0	10.8	10.8
Germany (Strassburg)	1907	1927	34.7	24.6	16.3
Denmark	1907	Still operating	59.0	74.5	67.0
Norway	1915	1938	60.0	53.6	50.4
The Netherlands	1916	1952	41.7	22.3	15.4
Finland	1917	Still operating	31.9	74.2	58.8
Sweden	1934	Still operating	64.6	81.0	65.2
Iceland	1955	Still operating	n.a.	89.1	90.7
Austria	1905-1907	1920	60.1	36.9	26.3

Source: Trade Union Dataset (oecd.org), https://stats.oecd.org/Index.aspx?DataSetCode=TUD and different other sources. 2 1979.

ces for the Nordic societies. The rapid mobilization of the working class brought about strong social-democratic parties that have played a central role in Scandinavian politics for more than a century. Strong unions have a particularly large influence on the workings of the Nordic labor markets, with their emphasis on labor market self-governance (cf. Chapter 5), but union clout also penetrates into many other policy areas. Employees and unions have a greater say in many political questions because strong unions are involved with decision-makers in many different areas, including education, health, and consumer questions.

Partisan relations to interest groups

For most of the twentieth century, early corporatism and the party systems of the Nordic countries largely mirrored the dominant structures of the industrial society. It is no surprise, then, that close ties existed between parties and the dominant interest groups. It is well known that the Nordic social-democratic parties had close and formal relations with the trade unions. These relations were curtailed in the late decades of the twentieth century, although more so in Denmark that in Norway and Sweden (Allern et al. 2007) – reflecting the fact that the Norwegian and Swedish social-democratic parties were comparatively stronger than the corresponding Danish party.

The other very close-knit party–class relationship was between the agrarian parties and the agricultural interest groups. This relation, which implied close formal and informal bonds, was strongest in Denmark, where the agricultural sector is comparatively stronger (Christiansen 2020). With the dramatic decline in rural populations, the agrarian parties have reoriented themselves, and are now also seeking to woo urban middle-class voters.

Groupings in the business community typically had close contact with conservative politicians, which in Denmark meant the Conservative Party. Today, they also have relations to *Venstre,* which, as just mentioned, has turned towards urban voters.

The golden age of corporatism

This section approaches the heyday of Nordic corporatism in two ways. First, it investigates one of the strongest institutional manifestations of corporatism: the integration of interest groups into the decision-making apparatus via commissions, committees, and councils. Second, it looks at the diffusion of corporatist structures into non-economic policy areas and into the running of public sector institutions.

Corporatism had its golden age in the three to four decades following World War II. Efforts to rebuild the Nordic economies after the war drew heavily on the close cooperation with business organizations and trade unions established during the economic crisis of the 1930s, and on the even closer cooperation that arose during the war. The early post-war decades were also characterized by heavy investments in publicly financed education and healthcare – similarly organized in close cooperation with industry and the trade unions – but additionally, at this point, with a prominent role for some of the large public sector trade unions. This golden age faded from the early 1980s onwards. Following the two oil crises in the 1970s, which caused significant changes in Western economies, governments were forced to introduce reforms that were not particularly compatible with the consensual policy-making so inherent in corporatism. Controversial reforms are difficult to adopt and implement in any consensual form, as also discussed in Chapter 7.

Inquiry commissions

In the early 1980s, as Lars Johansen and Ole P. Kristensen (1982: 196) observed, "there are reasons to believe that public committees have long since become one of the most important, if not the single most important, mode of interest intermediation." Commissions or inquiry commissions are ad hoc bodies set up with the purpose of preparing a political decision. Committees, on the other hand, are permanent bodies that perform administrative duties or act as advisory bodies to parliament or to a minister. Setting up committees that have interest group membership, and which prepare or implement public policies or advise government and parliament, makes interest groups an integrated part of the public decision-making machinery. These observations apply to all the Nordic countries.

Commissions and committees are used in many Western countries for the same purposes as in the Nordics. In the Nordic region, however, commissions and committees came to be used extensively, and interest groups became involved in the vast majority of these collective bodies. For a period, interest groups in Sweden even became part of the governance structure of the country's many politically independent public agencies. In the Nordic variants of the commission and committee system, unions play a much more prominent role than in most other countries, reflecting the high degree of unionization. A Danish-Swiss comparison showed that both countries have many commissions and committees that include interest group representatives, but there are relatively many union representatives in Denmark and very few in Switzerland (Christiansen, Mach, & Varone 2015). In addition, union representatives in the Nordics are typically more present in the system of public inquiry commissions and play a greater role in them than in most other countries.

As suggested earlier, commissions and committees come in many different forms. Policy inquiry commissions scrutinize a politically defined problem and propose solutions. During the twentieth century the Nordic countries produced thousands of commission reports on relatively unpoliticized topics, as well as on highly politicized issues such as social welfare and municipal amalgamations. Commissions are a multifaceted and multifunctional phenomenon (Hesstvedt & Christiansen 2022).

Box 3.1 tells the story of one Danish policy inquiry commission that is an extreme example of consensual policy-making. The resulting Technological Services Act reorganized the public infrastructure for technological service provision to private firms and also established the

Council for Technology. The process is related to a type of issue that is important to and engaging for the business community, but is not particularly interesting to elected politicians. Note that the Economic Council of the Labor Movement was represented in the commission. Of course this council also had views on business matters, but its presence was crucially a hint to the Social Democratic opposition that the labor movement's views would be given due consideration. This seems to have worked. The bill was passed in the Folketing with unanimous support from all political parties.

Box 3.1 The Technological Services Act 1973, Denmark

The Danish parliament, the Folketing, adopted the Technological Services Act in 1973. This law established a Council for Technology to advise the Danish government and the Folketing on business-related technological issues. More importantly for businesses, the law laid the foundation for establishing a number of publicly subsidized technological service institutions to help Danish companies overcome technological problems. In November 1970 – under a center-right government – a commission was established to work out a plan for organizing technological services in Denmark. This commission consisted of civil servants, representatives from business groups, the Danish Society of Engineers, the Danish Technological Institutes, the Technical Research Council, and the Economic Council of the Labor Movement. The commission's report, published in June 1972, largely followed the preferences of the Industrial Council and the Association of Metal Manufacturers, but its recommendations were unanimously endorsed by all members. After a consultation period and the subsequent parliamentary process, the Technological Services Act was passed on March 16, 1973. All parties in parliament voted in favor of the bill. The initiative to propose this legislation came from outside the state apparatus, the involvement of the relevant interest groups was substantial, and the political process added very little to the committee's proposal.

Source: Christiansen, Nørgaard, & Sidenius (2004)

Another example, also from Denmark, is the Welfare Reform Commission of 1964 (explained in Box 3.2), which worked on key administrative and financial issues, so its substance was of immense interest to the elected politicians. All political parties in the Folketing were represented in the commission, as were the partners from both sides of the labor market, and relevant public authorities. Even clients' organizations, such as the national association of people with disabilities, were represented. The commission worked for eight years before delivering its second report, entitled *Social Services and Social Welfare*, in 1972. However, the patience of the commission and stakeholders was rewarded, as many of the report's recommendations were adopted.

Box 3.2 The Welfare Reform Commission of 1964, Denmark

The Welfare Reform Commission was established in Denmark in 1964 under a Social Democratic-led government. Its purpose was to establish how to reform the administrative, organizational, and financial structure of the country's welfare system, which included preparing several legislative bills. Its 23 members included politicians from all parties in the Folketing, representatives from the employers' and employees' organizations, the local government organizations, clients' associations, the "sick-leave funds" of that era, and, obviously, the Ministry of Social Affairs. The commission's first report was published in 1969, its second in 1972. Many of the commission's recommended proposals were implemented in the years that followed, including a comprehensive reform of the welfare system that was passed into law in 1974.

Source: Christiansen & Nørgaard (2009)

The two commissions outlined in Boxes 3.1 and 3.2 are not representative of all commissions, but they largely reflect how political compromises are based on commission work that includes all interest groups with a stake in the issues under scrutiny. The Welfare Reform Commission even had representatives from all political parties, as noted. The societal backdrop of both commissions was a long period of prosperity, economic growth, development of public sector programs, and optimism in general. Social security programs were expanded, and only the most poorly organized taxpayers could reasonably protest. Around 1980, Denmark set up a total of 280 policy-preparing commissions, 188 of which had representatives from interest groups as members. Norway had 116 commissions in all, and 68 with interest group representation. Sweden had 83 commissions in all, only 16 with interest group representatives as members (Christiansen et al. 2010). This is probably because Swedish economic interest groups – particularly business and industry groups and trade unions – were integrated into the political machinery already through board membership in the various independent Swedish agencies (Rothstein 1992), and thus within the state apparatus. During the three decades after World War II, agencies with interest group representatives as board members grew from 28 to 74 percent. At the peak of this trend in Sweden, almost one out of three board members was an interest group representative.

Inquiry commissions are dismantled when their job is done – that is, when they have produced one or more white papers.[8] In addition to inquiry commissions, the Nordic countries also have various permanent committees. These typically come in three forms: First, there are *advisory* committees that assist a minister or parliament on a certain issue. These are often relatively large and typically embrace a plethora of relevant interests within their field. Other committees have *administrative* competence, for example supervising and managing an agricultural subsidy program. Finally, *appeals* boards hear and decide complaints from citizens, firms, and public authorities, looking at decisions made at lower administrative levels.

8. A white paper is a report issued by a government authority, often written by a commission tasked with scrutinizing and considering possible solutions to a political problem

All of these bodies have one thing in common: Parliament has accepted that they make decisions that accommodate the views of interest groups, thereby setting the stage for consensual processes to unfold.

Public sector corporatism

Early corporatism was a phenomenon solely related to labor market and industrial issues, and it paved the way for finding workable and legitimate solutions to problems of all scales. What is more, it also proved workable in handling issues related to the public sector. Besides economic recovery, the first three decades after World War II were especially dedicated to developing the educational system, along with healthcare and social services. In these processes, public sector unions came to play an important role in policy-making and implementation. In all the Nordic countries the trade unions in the public sector became integrated in the political-administrative machinery in the same way that private sector unions and business groups had become integrated in regulating the labor market and the industrial sector.

At the height of corporatism, public sector unions in the Nordics were believed to be quite influential both from the top down, and from the bottom up; both at the national political level, and in individual schools and public daycare institutions. This was due in large part to a well-developed shop steward system in publicly run workplaces. To this day, many Nordic public sector trade unions have extremely high membership, in some sectors close to 100 percent. Their strength is – or was – partly a consequence of the absence of significant market threats, which left more room for the unions to operate.

The heyday of Nordic corporatism

Nordic corporatism is not the result of wise thinkers or politicians foreseeing how their countries could develop in a peaceful, consensual way. Corporatism resulted from iterative efforts to solve societal problems that followed in the wake of the industrial society. These efforts, trial-and-error style, happened to take place in societies characterized by strong mobilization from the bottom up, where the not-so-well-off could use their strength in numbers and their internal unity to better their situation. While corporatism was well suited to industrial societies and conflicts, it became a millstone around the neck of Western societies, also in the Nordic region, when they suddenly found themselves facing new challenges in the 1970s.

The next chapter is devoted to the current state of Nordic corporatism, but before moving on I have several relevant observations to make on the present-day effects of the Nordic corporatist tradition.

For one thing, Nordic corporatism has been an integral part of the relatively consensual Nordic societies. Giving interest group access to political and administrative decision-making has eased potential tensions between the political administrative elite and the people. The Nordic countries are not harmonious heavens devoid of disputes, but societal, cultural, economic, and political problems are handled in less conflictual ways than in many other countries.

Nordic corporatism is also typified by the trade unions' prominent role, and by the countries' relatively strong social-democratic parties. These have influenced labor market policies (see Chapter 5) and many other policy areas as well. By giving union representatives access to many arenas where other policies are discussed, Nordic policies overall represent a stronger balance of business interests vis-à-vis other interests in society, keeping business interests from dominating as much as they do in some other countries.

Such balancing of society's interests is also found in environmental policy. Modern Nordic environmental policy is only 50 years old, but it too is typified by corporatist structures. The Nordic countries have numerous environmental organizations, some of which play a significant role in formulating and implementing environmental policies. This is another example of policies that are more balanced than in many other countries (Christiansen 1996).

The last point I will make here is that the corporatist legacy – almost independently of the status of present-day corporatism – has left the Nordic countries with very strong interest groups, which corporatism not only presupposes but also produces. Close interaction with the government machinery enables special interest groups to give their members first-class services and advice on public regulations: How should a regulation be interpreted, and what is in the pipeline from the government? And the Nordics not only have strong unions; they also have strong business groups. Almost all Nordic private companies are members of one or more business groups, and the organization rate is 100 percent for companies ranging in size from just a handful of employees upwards. What is more, corporatism has paved the way for strong interest groups in other parts of society. For example, interest groups played a significant role in the comparatively successful handling of the COVID-19 pandemic in the Nordic region. In Denmark, 85 committees were established with a total of 1,341 members, 600 of whom were from interest groups, 122 from private firms, and 619 from the civil services and public sector (Christiansen 2020). In many ways, strong interest groups can be a valuable resource for a society, but they can also pose a challenge when the preferences of the elected politicians deviate from the views of strong interest groups, as the cases outlined later, in Chapter 7, will show.

Chapter 4.

Privileged pluralism

In the mid-1960s the Norwegian political scientist Stein Rokkan described his country's governance system with the following catchphrase: "Votes count, resources decide." What he meant was that the corporatist channel, populated by interest groups and bureaucrats, was more powerful than the parliamentary channel populated by voters and elected politicians. While the statement exaggerated the relationship between the two channels, it contained some truth: In certain policy areas, powerful interest groups had won very strong positions both in policy formulation and implementation. Elected politicians and civil servants were not free to guide the Nordic countries in the directions they preferred – should they wish to pursue a course not endorsed by the most powerful unions and business groups. This is no longer the case.

Many scholars and political scientists have declared that corporatism is weakened, even dead, or at the very least unconscious (Crepaz 1992; Christiansen & Rommetvedt 1999). Based on what we know, however, this diagnosis is premature (Christiansen 2020). Interest groups still play an important role in Nordic policy-making and implementation. As corporatist structures expanded throughout most of the twentieth century, interest groups grew even stronger. While corporatism presupposes strong interest groups, it also breeds them. And if corporatism is all about the integration of privileged interest groups in forming and implementing policy, then we still see clear elements of corporatism in the Nordic countries. Meanwhile, it is true that corporatism has changed. In the following sections we investigate how interest group involvement in political decision-making takes place today, and why.

Adaptation of Scandinavian corporatism

One group of scholars has relabeled privileged corporatism, now calling it "privileged pluralism" (Binderkrantz, Christiansen, & Pedersen 2014). This stresses that while there are still different classes of interest groups in terms of access and privilege, the range of interest groups has diversified, for example with the growth of civil society groups, some of which have significant political influence.

Table 4.1 lists some of the key changes from corporatism classic to the modern-day Scandinavian model, now labeled *privileged pluralism.* In the following, I will outline the role of interest groups in consensual policy-making. The theoretical lens through which we will observe these changes is the model of *political exchange*, presented in Figure 3.1, which shows how the influence of interest groups is exchanged for information and political support. The model captures important parts of the interplay between the state and interest groups, showing that changes in this relationship must be accompanied by changes in the political exchanges that go on between the state and the interest groups.

A classic aspect of Nordic corporatism is its extensive mediation of special interests. Strong interest groups are influential players in most policy areas, and they are more or less automatically involved when their interests

Table 4.1 The adaptation of Scandinavian corporatism

	Classic Scandinavian corporatism	**Modern Scandinavian corporatism: privileged pluralism**
Nature of interest mediation	Encompassing	Partial
Policy-making	Commissions, privileging logic	Ministerial preparation, less privileging logic
Resources supplied by groups	Technical and political support implementation	Technical and political information, implementation
State autonomy	Low	High
Types of interest represented	Abundance of economic groups, few citizens' groups	Abundance of economic groups, more citizens' groups
Relevant actors	Interest groups, civil servants, elected politicians	Interest groups, large firms, thinktanks, public affairs firms, the media, civil servants, elected politicians

Source: Adapted from Binderkrantz & Christiansen (2015)

are at stake. Some scholars have even talked about a *principle of affected interests*, according to which interest groups potentially affected by a proposal have the right to be consulted before a decision is made, and even in such good time that they can actually oppose it if they want to (Christiansen 1999). Classic Nordic corporatism was quite close to living up to this standard. Although this may still be an ideal today, in practice interest groups play a less crucial role, and in some cases even normally privileged interest groups are not invited to discuss a proposal. An example of this would be certain labor market reforms, which are discussed below.

The role of policy inquiry commissions

One way to approach the changing role of interest groups is to look at how laws are processed today compared to in the classic corporatist model. One major change is that the use of policy inquiry commissions has declined considerably in the Nordic countries since the 1970s.

Although the political logic of the commission system in the three Scandinavian countries is quite similar – to prepare public policies in accordance with different considerations in order to enhance efficiency and legitimacy – there are also some differences. The commission system was used far more in Sweden than in the other two countries. For a couple of years in the 1990s, the Swedes produced nearly 200 commission reports yearly. One explanation is that the Swedish system uses commission work in cases where Denmark and Norway would choose, for instance, to have an in-house report prepared. Many Swedish commission reports are written by a single person, often a university academic, and they are the functional equivalents of Danish or Norwegian policy preparation documents made within the country's ministerial hierarchy. Single-author reports are much less resource intensive than commission reports written by a group of individuals who represent different perspectives on the topic, and who have different interests in the outcome.

Table 4.2 shows the number of Danish active decision-preparing commissions and committees at the end of each five-year period. In 1985, Denmark had no fewer than 168 commissions doing preparatory work on political and administrative decisions, and 118 of these had members from interest groups. Five years later, only 78 commissions were left, 57 with interest group representation. By the end of 2020 the inventory list only counted 15 policy inquiry commissions, 10 of which had representatives from interest groups.

Table 4.2 Public committees in Denmark, selected years 1985–2020. Numbers in total, and committees with interest group members in parentheses

	1985	1990	2000	2010	2015	2020
Total number of commissions and committees	516 (394)	388 (319)	513 (376)	436 (315)	412 (296)	369 (306)
Policy inquiry commissions	168 (118)	78 (57)	92 (55)	44 (27)	19 (13)	15 (10)
Administrative committees	153 (114)	128 (104)	195 (129)	192 (132)	169 (117)	187 (129)
Advisory committees	195 (152)	182 (158)	226 (192)	200 (156)	224 (166)	167 (159)

Source: Christiansen & Nørgaard (2003, updated)

Inquiry commissions are still used, but less frequently than before, even if the Swedish numbers are still relatively high. This means that interest groups' preferences must be accommodated in different ways than before, if they are accommodated at all. Nowadays, preparing political decisions is much more a matter for civil servants in the ministries. They control the processes, from ideation to full policy proposal. Interest groups are by no means absent from these processes, but their involvement is different now. Where a seat in a policy inquiry commission makes you a close partner who has detailed information on the strategy and tactics of the other actors, present-day policy preparation depends more on the preferences of civil servants and ministers, which means less precise knowledge about the process for interest groups. To put it rather bluntly, the conditions for special interest organizations in the political exchange – the give and take – are now more rigorous. Referring back to Figure 3.1: If you can deliver relevant information and political support, you are most welcome. If not, your gaining access to the decision-making arena is less likely. This means that the will and efforts made to accommodate affected stakeholders has lessened, as discussed below.

While inquiry commissions are still widely used, administrative hearings have become mandatory: Before a political proposal enters the parliamentary stage it is sent for consultation and comments to other public authorities, interest groups, and experts. The details may vary among the Nordics, but the main point is that affected stakeholders have a chance to comment on political proposals. Their comments are published, along with responses from the relevant ministers. What takes place after a proposal is revealed is therefore much more transparent than what happens between an idea being conceived and a proposal being ready for an administrative consultation round.

The downside from the interest groups' viewpoint is that the consultation is opened at a very late stage in the decision-making process, so typically very little opportunity for agency remains. Figure 4.1 is a stylized presentation of the relationship between the *room for agency* and the *time elapsed* since the initial idea for a proposal is conceived. It takes great effort and mobilization – and most likely some luck as well – to change a government proposal dramatically at this late stage. Responding to a proposal in a consultation round often does pay off though. Danish data show that nearly 30 percent of all consultation responses are followed by a full or partial concession from the ministry, which then changes the proposal accordingly (Binderkrantz & Christiansen 2023).

Administrative corporatism, meaning the presence of special interest groups in advisory and administrative bodies, has not followed the same development as the policy-preparing commissions. In Denmark there are more administrative committees today than in the 1980s, and advisory committees are at the same level today as in the

Figure 4.1 Agency room and time, stylized representation

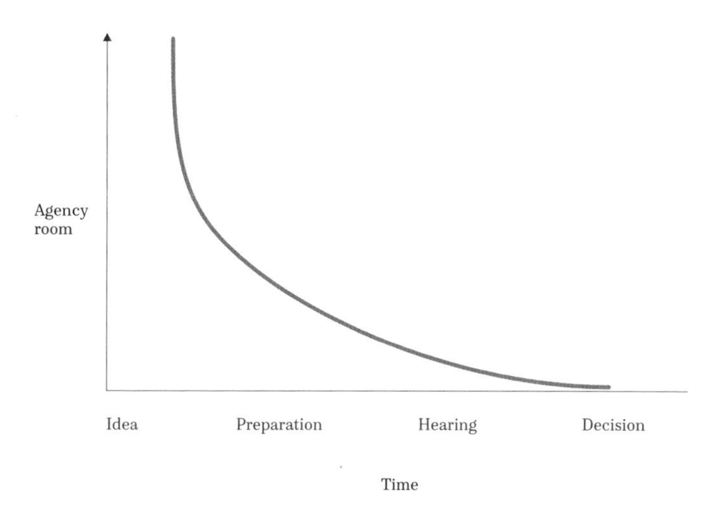

1980s. The changes in the political exchange relationship are primarily related to policy formation and less to policy administration, if that has even changed at all.

What are the reasons for this? Relying on policy inquiry commissions to formulate public policies comes with some disadvantages. First, commission work takes time. It takes time to establish the tasks for the commission, and to agree on the terms, find members, deliberate, compromise, and finally write the report. Then it takes time to digest the report, and to translate it into practical political proposals that must be treated in new negotiations in parliament before a bill may be passed into law. Commission work can easily take two to four years, including the time taken to set up the commission at the start, and to operationalize its suggestion or recommendations at the end. Such a timespan may not be acceptable to politicians who want to see results before the next election. There is a growing awareness of the clash between *high-speed society* and *low-speed democracy* (Kersbergen & Vis 2022).

It is not difficult to make the theoretical argument that if actors with diverging preferences must find a consensual solution to a specific problem, the result will fall within the acceptance zone for all participating actors. This seems to have been possible in the numerous cases in which public policy in the Nordic countries has been endorsed by interest groups – even groups with conflicting interests – during the build-up of policies to support labor market regimes, and of industrial policies and welfare policies developed after World War II for health, education, and social affairs. The main reason is that there has always been something in it for everyone. However, with changing political agendas, meaning governments may pursue reforms that imply costs to otherwise privileged actors, policy inquiry commissions are a less valuable means of political compromise: How do you persuade people to be part of a commission that will be asked to come up with proposals that will mean cuts for their members? The answer is simple: You don't try because you can't.

Overall, this means that the involvement of interest groups in the political exchange has changed somewhat. Their classic role, in which they are expected to deliver technical information and political support, and play a part in implementing the results, has been replaced by a more distant relationship with state actors. In other words, state actors have gained rather more autonomy vis-à-vis interest groups. At the same time the policy process has also become more complex, with the advent of new actors.

New actors

Traditionally, Nordic corporatism was heavily based on interest groups and their privileged access to political decision-making. Political decisions came into being in a segmented system consisting of interest groups, civil servants, and elected politicians. Large interest groups are still important political players today. They are still privileged, and they still contribute to consensual conflict resolution and consensual policy-making. However, they also work in a much more complex environment. In the current special interest landscape of the Nordics, the many associations in civil society tend to play a more prominent role, in line with the rise of new political issues that are less related to economic questions.

From the 1970s onwards, new actors have been trying to enter the political theater. Some large private corporations were, and are, increasingly politically active, in addition to being members of interest groups. This is new in societies like the Nordics, which have such a strong corporatist legacy. For one thing, thinktanks[9] are on the rise as actors pursuing political influence. They have much in common with interest groups, although many of them are more idea-based, and some have an explicit center-right or center-left affiliation. Public affairs companies that offer services to firms or special interest organizations and help to formulate and disseminate political messages to the public, or to decision-makers, are also growing in number. Finally, the media – printed, electronic, and social – have come to play a very prominent role in the strategies of interest groups and other actors seeking to shape the political agenda and political decisions. Overall, the policy-making landscape has become much more complicated in the past 50 years or so.

9. Thinktanks are organized policy professionals who analyze and provide solutions to social, political, or economic issues. They are often affiliated with political parties and/or ideologies

"The Northern lights"

The American political scientist Mancur Olson (1932-1998) was one of the world's most influential interest group scholars by virtue of his theoretical work on collective action, and on why, in many cases, it is not rational for actors to invest in collective goods. His book *The Rise and Decline of Nations* (1990) showed that national wealth was inversely related to the strength of interest groups. In his view, special interest groups are simply interested in getting a bigger piece of the pie, not in increasing the size of pie. However, the Scandinavian countries did not fit into that theory. They were more prosperous than they should have been, considering their strong interest groups. Olson invented a special explanation for the economic success of Scandinavia: the existence of what he termed "encompassing" groups. These groups – notably the trade unions – were so large that they had rational reasons to care about the size of the pie. He was later invited to Sweden, and after studying the country and the region he published a book in which he asked: "How bright are the Northern Lights?" His answer was: "I believe there really are Northern Lights. They are beautiful (...) But they are not bright or stable enough to save a society, if it rushes far ahead without taking along any further sources of light, from stumbling into catastrophe" (Olson 1990: 69).

Olson saw that Scandinavian corporatism had in fact brought wealth and growth to the region, but he also saw that relying solely on corporatist decision-making could get a country into big trouble. That was precisely what Scandinavian decision-makers themselves had come to realize around 1990, the year Olson's book was published.

Corporatism has survived in the Nordic countries, but in a softer version that leaves more autonomy to state actors. Corporatism still glues the region's societies together, with political decisions reached in a way that promotes consensual processes. At the same time, however, elected governments have gained the autonomy to make decisions that benefit wider interests in society, rather than the narrower interests of influential groups or organizations.

Chapter 5.

The Nordic labor market model

Societies face many types of conflicts. Among the most important are disputes related to the labor market. Labor markets are vital for the economy and thus for society as a whole; they are also important for companies and for individuals. How does a national labor market react to international shifts? What are the salary levels for different jobs? How are employees protected, and who must bear the costs of unemployment – the jobless, or society as a whole, or some model in between? How can workplaces ensure a safe working environment? Well-functioning labor markets depend on institutions that enable companies and individuals to respond to external threats and take advantage of new opportunities. Inflexible labor markets lead to lock-ins, situations with idle labor resources, and lost opportunities. This chapter is devoted to explaining how the Nordic countries handle labor market conflicts. Previous chapters have already touched on the origins of the Nordic labor market model; here, we look at the current labor market model and how it works.

Scholars who study the Nordic countries often find that traits which appear very similar from a distance often veil major differences. This is also true of the Nordic labor markets. On the surface they look quite alike: high wage levels, low wage dispersion, high employment ratios, strong unions, Ghent-type systems (except in Norway), flexibility, high insurance benefits, few precarious jobs, and so forth. But a closer look reveals that their institutions vary, and so do their outcomes in some respects. This has caused some researchers to conclude that there is no common model for the labor markets in the Nordics (Gooderham et al. 2015). Nevertheless, there are some common features that justify the idea of a common Nordic model.

Looking at the Nordic labor markets from a distance, we can identify two common traits. The first is *self-regulation* by the social partners, given that many aspects regulated by law in most Western countries are regulated in the Nordics through collective agreements between employers and trade unions. Labor market conflicts are therefore primarily a matter for the labor market actors to handle, and national bodies only step in if this process fails.

The second trait is *flexicurity*, a high level of both flexibility and security (seen in most of the Nordic labor markets and explained in more depth later). This principle makes it easy to hire and fire employees, at least compared to in many other countries, such as France, the Netherlands, Spain, and Japan. Unemployment benefits are generous and relatively accessible, which means that the level of income compensation for jobless workers is high. In addition, the Nordic countries run active labor market policies, including providing supplementary education and upskilling programs at different levels for large groups in the labor market (Jensen 2017).

Generally speaking, the Nordic labor market institutions must also be seen in the context of the universal Nordic welfare state, with its emphasis on publicly financed or subsidized welfare services. These include education, childcare, and tax-financed healthcare, all of which support broad labor market participation (Esping-Andersen 1993; Høgedahl 2020).

Self-regulation

The self-regulating labor market model is seen in slightly different guises across the Nordic countries. It is particularly strong in Denmark and Sweden, and less pronounced in Finland and Norway. The core principle is that a large part of all relevant labor market issues and disputes are settled through agreements between the "social partners", meaning representatives of the two sides sitting at the bargaining table: employers and employees. This leaves a less prominent role for legal regulation via parliament. The self-regulating model presupposes several things (Høgedahl 2020):

1. A well-organized labor market with strong trade unions and strong employer organizations.

2. Regular (re)negotiation of labor market agreements on salary and working conditions, and a state-driven conciliation body that can be mobilized to mediate if employers and employees disagree, and whose decisions are respected by the social partners.

3. A consensual negotiating atmosphere between the social partners, and a relatively low level of conflict.

The self-regulating model leaves the Nordic countries with a delimitation that is different from most other countries in terms of what is regulated by the social partners and what is regulated by the national parliaments. In the case of Denmark, typically the social partners negotiate "collective agreements" – sets of conditions that are valid for two or three years – which employers and employees will adhere to for the agreed period. Such collective agreements regulate salaries, working hours, the rights and duties of senior employees, pensions, notices of termination, and other relevant issues. Certain types of collective agreements leave some issues to be settled at a local level. Other issues, including holidays and parental leave, are regulated at a national level by law.

Three Nordic countries – Denmark, Finland, and Sweden – are members of the European Union (EU). EU regulations frequently contradict the Scandinavian self-regulating models, particularly parts of EU's social regulatory framework (Arnholtz 2022). In some cases EU regulations have been implemented through collective agreements in Nordic EU member states, meaning without the involvement of political regulation. One recent EU policy caused a particularly intense conflict between the Danish and Swedish governments on the one side and the EU on the other: the question of minimum wage. Denmark, Finland, and Sweden do not have any official minimum wages set by law. Even so, their de facto minimum wages are significantly higher than the official wages in EU countries that have a legally stipulated minimum wage because they have been set by collective bargaining.

When, in 2020, the EU Commission proposed introducing official minimum wages throughout the EU, the Danish and Swedish governments protested, arguing that minimum wages would undermine the Nordic self-regulatory model. The trade unions were especially forceful in protesting against introducing a minimum wage (Arnholtz 2022). They feared it would squeeze their membership even more: Why should people care about union membership if one of the most important elements of any employment contract, one's wages, was secured by national legislation and not through trade-union membership? The EU's minimum wage proposal was passed in 2022, although with a promise from the EU Commission's president, Ursula von der Leyen, that the regulation would not damage the Danish, Finnish, or Swedish models. The potential effects remain to be seen.

For the model to work in practice, employers and employees must both be well organized. In many countries this is the case for employers, but with considerable variation (Martin & Swank 2012). However, there is even more variation in the strength and level of employee organization. The Nordic countries, with the partial exception of Norway, are the odd ones out in this respect, having unionization rates well above 60 percent. Outside the Nordic countries, only Belgium has a similar level (as also mentioned in Chapter 4). Without a certain power and resource balance between employers and employees, the model is too vulnerable for the less powerful side: How can the weaker side be sure that the other side will fully respect the collective agreement they reach? This reason alone makes it difficult, perhaps even impossible, to export the Nordic model successfully to countries with significantly weaker trade unions.

Flexicurity

Returning to the term *flexicurity,* and its constituent elements of *flexibility* and *security*: The flexibility lies in employees' relatively low protection against being fired, and the security lies in the availability of generous and easily accessible unemployment benefits. In addition to flexibility and security, flexicurity includes an active labor market policy component that aims to match supply and demand in the labor market, for example through education, retraining, upskilling, and other measures. As pointed out by Cathie Jo Martin (2018), the Nordic model of education (*dannelse* in Danish, along the lines of the German *Bildung* tradition) implies a focus on skills and academic learning, as well as on fostering individuals who are well versed in the workings of society and in cultural history.

The unemployment benefits aspect of the flexicurity system provides an explanation for why there is not much protection against firing in the Nordic countries, where strong unions and social-democratic parties would be supposed to push legislation in favor of union preferences. Compared to many other countries, the Nordics have unemployment benefits that are both generous and available for relatively long periods. In France, for example, the level of protection against being fired is high, but this is a negative inducement to employers to hire, since it becomes costly to dispose of idle labor. On several occasions the French president Emmanuel Macron has pointed to the Nordic labor markets as models for his vision of France. However, it is not easy to import such policies from countries that work differently. In the case of Denmark, the model turned out to be insufficiently robust until the "easy hire, easy fire" model was supplemented by active labor market policies during the 1990s. Today, the Nordic recipe for robustness is flexibility, security, and active labor market policies.

A closer look at the four largest Nordic countries (leaving Iceland out) reveals some differences: Denmark is considered to have the most far-reaching flexicurity system, though with a reduced level of security instruments during the last two decades (as discussed below). Sweden has a less flexible model, obliged by law to apply a "last in, first out" rule when terminating employees. Norway and Finland are somewhere in between (Heggebø 2016).

Protection against firing is also structured very differently. In Denmark, eligibility for unemployment benefits requires membership of, and payment to, an unemployment fund, and two years' employment. Those eligible can receive 90 percent of their prior salary, but with a low cap amount. In 2022, an unemployed Dane could receive a monthly maximum of 19,351 DKK, equivalent to 2,580 Euros. The low cap means that the actual compensation rate for most employees is significantly lower than 90 percent; it is 50 percent or less for many recipients. After a maximum of two years on benefits, a recipient must work a normal job for two years before earning the right to another two-year unemployment period (www.borger.dk).

From a trade union perspective, the Danish arrangement has gradually deteriorated in recent decades in terms of the benefit period, the conditions for renewing eligibility, and the size of benefits. During the same period, however, the minimum unemployment level in Denmark – often called "structural unemployment" – has dropped from just over 10 percent to around 3 percent.

On the face of it, the Norwegian benefit system looks less generous, but in practice it is more generous for most benefit recipients. Norway does not apply a Ghent system, so Norwegian employees need not be a member of an unemployment fund. Unemployed people receive 62.2 percent of their previous income for up to two years. However, the Norwegian cap is much higher than the Danish cap, which means that the compensation rate is also higher for unemployed people with a higher previous income. The Swedish system is closer to the Danish than to the Norwegian system, because Sweden, like Denmark, adheres to the Ghent system.

Flexicurity makes sense for viable labor markets with a high capacity to adapt to external shocks, to which small economies are particularly vulnerable. External shocks and economic crises are more easily overcome with flexible firing and hiring. For instance, the Nordic countries withstood the COVID-19 pandemic better than many others. This was not only because their economies were sound when the pandemic hit; it was also because they had instruments, used for running a flexible labor market, that could easily be adapted to pandemic-imposed circumstances (Greve et al. 2021).

Flexicurity is also highly valued in industries such as fishery and agriculture, which depend on the weather and other rapidly changing conditions. Employees sometimes find themselves in and out of a job from one day to the next. Again, the question is: Who should bear the cost of idle labor? In the flexicurity model, costs are borne by the unemployment funds, with the state as a prime sponsor supplementing the membership fees.

It should be added that the flexicurity model goes hand in hand with many other rights for employees, despite the ease of firing. The only particularly liberal feature is the weak protection against firing. In many respects, labor is expensive in the Nordic model, as employees have achieved many rights over the years. Generous vacation rules, for example, and generous rights to parental leave, are protected by law. So is the working environment, which is generally healthy and safe in the Nordics. These employee rights (many of which apply to all citizens) are envied in many other countries. For instance, health insurance and a basic old-age pension are not related to a person's labor market performance but are universal rights – a key element in the Nordic welfare state models.

The employer organizations and the trade unions not only accept the flexicurity model; they also have a say in its construction (Høgedahl 2020). Workers' and employers' rights, protection against being fired, and unemployment systems and benefits are core issues for the social partners, and for many decades they have been deeply involved in creating and developing the Nordic labor market model. They also discuss the details of the policy instruments of the model: Should it be harder to fire employees? Are unemployment benefits and the conditions for obtaining them too generous? Despite these recurring discussions, the system has earned a high level of support from the public at large, and also among the social partners. But what are the effects of the Nordic labor markets, and how do they compete with other systems?

Effects of the Nordic labor market model

The *unemployment rate* is one of the most important indicators of how healthy a labor market is. Unemployment is affected by many factors, one of which is the

Table 5.1 Annual unemployment rates in selected countries, 2005-2021

	2005	2006	2007	2008	2009	2010	2011	2012	2013	2014	2015	2016	2017	2018	2019	2020	2021
Denmark	4.8	3.9	3.8	3.7	6.4	7.8	7.8	7.8	7.4	6.9	6.3	6.0	5.8	5.1	5.1	5.7	5.1
Finland	8.4	7.7	6.9	6.4	8.4	8.5	8,0	7.8	8.3	8.8	9.5	8.9	8.8	7.4	6.7	7.7	7.7
Norway	4.5	3.6	2.7	3.0	3.5	4.0	3.6	3.5	3.4	3.8	4.7	5.0	4.4	4.0	3.9	4.8	4.5
Sweden	7.8	7.2	6.3	6.4	8.5	8.8	8.0	8.1	8.2	8.1	7.6	7.2	6.9	6.5	7.0	8.5	8.8
France	8.9	8.9	8.0	7.4	9.1	9.3	9.2	9.8	10.3	10.3	10.4	10.1	9.4	9.0	8.4	8.0	7.9
The Netherlands	7.0	6.1	5.3	4.8	5.4	6.1	6.1	6.8	8.2	8.4	7.9	7.0	5.9	4.9	4.4	4.9	4.2
US	5.0	4.6	4.6	5.8	9.3	9.6	9.00	8.0	7.4	6.2	5.3	4.9	4.4	4.0	3.7	8.1	5.4
UK	4.8	5.4	5.3	5.7	7.6	7.9	8.1	8.0	7.6	6.1	5.4	5.0	4.4	4.1	3.8	4.6	4.5

Source: Unemployment rate (oecd.org), https://data.oecd.org/unemp/unemployment-rate.htm

national labor market. Table 5.1 shows the unemployment rates in selected countries between 2005 and 2021. Over this long period, we can see how the labor market relates to the business cycle. The Nordic countries fare well, although not exceptionally well, in comparison with the other countries shown. Denmark starts and ends at the low end but was severely affected by the economic crisis after the financial crisis of 2008–2009. Norway had very little unemployment throughout the period, probably due to its exceptionally strong economy, which is fueled by revenues from the booming oil sector. Finland and Sweden have fairly stable unemployment rates but at higher levels than Denmark and Norway, and in general they fare worse than the Netherlands, the UK, and the US.

The conclusion on unemployment is that the Nordic model performs well, but some other countries still perform much better than certain Nordic countries.

Industrial action is another relevant measure to consider. With the Nordic focus on consensus, social partners, and collective negotiations, one might expect these systems to be more or less strike free. That is not the case, as Table 5.2 shows. Finland lost a large number of workdays to strikes in 1990, as did Norway in 2010, and Sweden in 1990. However, no Nordic countries are close to reaching the French level. On the other hand, no Nordic countries have a total during these three years as low as Germany or the US. It is clear that a labor market based on negotiations between the social partners is no guarantee against strikes. A probable explanation for the varying strike rates in the Nordics is that because unionization is high, strikes become quite comprehensive when they finally do occur.

Moving on to *precarious jobs*, there is no official definition of this term, but there seems to be a consensus that it covers temporary jobs, often not full time, with lower pay and fewer rights than standard jobs offer, such as health insurance or holiday pay. Precarious jobs – includ-

Table 5.2 Annual average of workdays lost to strikes per 1,000 salaried employees

	1990	2010	2015
Denmark	41	8	52
Finland	444	60	52
Norway	79	217	10
Sweden	189	7	2
Germany	2	1	31
France	727	318	81
UK	304	15	3
US	73	2	5

Source: OECD Collective Bargaining in OECD and accession countries (www.oecd.org/els/emp/Industrial-disputes.pdf)

ing seasonal ones – are found in many trades, including food delivery, restaurants, bars, hotels, and agriculture. Workers in such jobs are rarely organized in trade unions and are a far cry from the ideal employees in the Nordic labor market model. Since trade unions oppose precarious labor arrangements, one would expect the Nordics to have few precarious jobs, while countries with weak unions could be expected to have many, but the picture is not that simple. The lack of a clear definition and the problems of delimiting precarious jobs in labor market statistics call for caution when we consider the numbers in Table 5.3. Having said this, it seems reasonable to conclude that a Nordic-style labor market model does not prevent precarious jobs (note Sweden and Finland), nor does the absence of a Nordic model mean that a country cannot have a small share of precarious jobs (note the UK and Germany).

Table 5.3 Precarious jobs as a share of the general workforce, selected countries, for 2009 and 2021

	2009	2021 (or most recent prior to 2021)
Denmark	1.2	1.2
Finland	3.3	3.5
Norway	0.7	0.7
Sweden	4.7	3.4
Germany	0.7	0.3 (2019)
France	4.3	4.9
The Netherlands	1.0	0.7
UK	0.4	0.3 (2019)

Source: "Precarious employment by sex, age and NACE Rev. 2 activity", Eurostat, http://appsso.eurostat.ec.europa.eu/nui/submitViewTableAction.do

We also measure *income inequality*, which is the result of many factors: the way the country's labor market works, the tax system, and the social welfare system, to mention a few. With strong unions one would expect that particularly low-paid jobs are relatively better paid in the Scandinavian countries. Because labor market income is a very large part of total incomes, one would also expect the Scandinavian countries to have more equal income distribution than most other countries.

There are several ways to measure income inequality (Jensen 2021). One of the most common is with the *Gini coefficient*, which measures the share of all income in a country that would have to be transferred from the highest-earning to the lowest-earning citizens to achieve total equality. The higher a country's Gini coefficient, the more unequal it is. Table 5.4 shows this coefficient for several countries over time. One thing to notice is that inequality has been on the rise since the early 1980s in most countries. However, this is not the case in France, where inequality was already high in 1981, or in the Netherlands, where inequality is among the lowest in the sample. Inequality is low in the Nordics – highest in Sweden, lowest in Finland – and significantly lower overall than in Germany, France, the UK, or the US, with the Nordics hovering around the same low level as the Netherlands.

To the extent that there is a causal relation between the way the labor market works and a country's level of inequality, the conclusion is that the Nordic labor market model reduces income inequality, though not in an exceptional way. Some other countries, such as the Netherlands, also produce a comparatively low level of inequality.

Table 5.4 Gini coefficients in selected countries for selected years

	1981 (or nearest year)	2000 (or nearest year)	2021
Denmark	.262	.238	.281
Finland	.222	.272	.273
Norway	.246 (1986)	.274	.276
Sweden	.229	.272	.297
Germany	.292	.288	.317
France	.369 (1984)	.311	.324
The Netherlands	.284	.281 (1999)	.281
UK	.319 (1986)	.384	.351
US	.374 (1986)	.401	.414

Source: Income inequality, Our World in Data (dataset), https://ourworldindata.org/grapher/economic-inequality-gini-index

The final measure of the possible effects of the Nordic labor market model examined here is the *satisfaction* of people who live within different labor market systems. Szczepaniak & Szvic-Obloza (2021) show that a high score on job satisfaction goes together with a high score on overall life satisfaction in the Nordic countries - as is also the case in some other countries such as Austria, Estonia, and Belgium. It is reasonable to see the high Nordic scores as an effect of the Nordic labor market model. Good working conditions and relatively high wages, even for low-wage earners, probably add to job satisfaction. Since one's job is so important for one's wellbeing, it is not strange that there is a correlation between job satisfaction and overall life satisfaction. With around 40 percent indicating high job satisfaction, there is room for improvement in the Scandinavian countries, but there is even more room in most other countries.

Here, we reach the same type of conclusion as we have for several other possible effects of the Nordic labor market model. The model fares well in terms of job satisfaction and life satisfaction – just as it did in terms of low unemployment, lost working days due to strikes, few precarious jobs, and comparatively low inequality – but so do some other countries. The Nordics have found a productive way to organize their labor markets, which is well suited to preconditions there. However, a few other small countries also do well, at least if we apply the above-mentioned factors as a standard.

The labor market model under pressure

The Nordic labor market model is under pressure from a couple of trends, which are best captured in terms of declining union membership. As mentioned above, the Nordic labor market model presupposes strong unions and strong employer organizations. And as shown in Table

Table 5.5 Trade union membership as a percentage in the Nordic countries, 2000 and 2019

	2000	2019
Denmark	74.5	67.0
Finland	74.2	58.8
Norway	53.6	50.4
Sweden	81.6	65.2

5.5, trade union membership in Denmark, Finland, Norway, and Sweden has decreased since 2000.

There are several reasons for this development. The trade union movement mobilized alongside industrialization and developed a strong class consciousness among the Nordic working classes. Today, blue-collar jobs are only a small fraction of total employment, and the traditional working-class mindset has vanished. Individualization, internationalization, and immigration have also squeezed trade union membership. Cuts in unemployment compensation rates have made the Ghent system for unemployment administration less attractive for high-wage earners. Whatever the exact reason, the trade unions have not succeeded in convincing new generations of employees that union membership makes it worth paying your dues.

The Nordic trade unions are still strong players in the Nordic labor markets, and they still have enough resources to be influential on the political scene, yet there is a limit to how many members they can lose before their value in the labor market, and in the political sphere, is significantly diminished. If the trade unions are severely weakened, this may affect issues that lie outside the labor market, for example the balance between the interests of businesses on one side and ordinary consumers on the other, to the disadvantage of the latter.

Chapter 6.

Voters, political parties, and parliamentary consensus-building

The Nordic countries have a tradition of minority governments, particularly after World War II. This is a consequence of their proportional voting systems and low thresholds for parliamentary representation, combined with the advent of many new parties and the fact that the government does not need a qualified majority to rule. But how are minority governments capable of governing stable and prosperous societies? And why are many bills adopted under such governments passed unanimously or with super-majorities, with more parties voting in favor of a bill than is strictly needed to adopt it? The fact is that in Scandinavia, not much legislation is passed with the absolute minimum of parliamentary votes required.

Consensual Nordic politics is a consequence of the difficult prospects for forming majority governments, which in turn is a consequence of the way the electoral systems and the parliamentary systems work, and the incentives they produce. In Scandinavia, elected politicians and parties act according to the rules and conditions under which they work (Green-Pedersen & Skjæveland 2020). Over the years, however, consensual policy-making has also become a valued norm in the region. Many voters prefer cooperative governments. Broad coalitions are said to be preferred over pure bloc politics, but when it comes to controversial issues or tough reforms, no bloc will hesitate to use a narrow majority if it has to.

Consensual policy-making has various advantages. Such decisions satisfy a broader set of stakeholder interests and leave minorities with a better chance of being heard. In addition, the risk of stop-and-go policies due to changes in parliamentary majorities is reduced. Consensual policy-making also produces more political stability than majoritarian systems, and stability is valued, even demanded, by many voters and businesses. Consensual policy-making brings the Scandinavian systems closer to Arend Lijphart's (1999) "kinder and more gentle democracy", but it also comes at a cost. One disadvantage is less clarity of responsibility, because broad majorities make it difficult for citizens to hold governments and parties responsible (Hobolt, Tilley, & Banducci 2013). Another is that it tends to create linear policy changes and may prevent necessary reforms (as will be described in Chapter 7).

In order to understand how the consensual Nordic systems work, we will review their electoral systems, party systems, and parliamentary policy-making systems.

Electoral systems

As pointed out by Lijphart (1999), proportional electoral systems correlate with consensual democracy. Such systems seldom produce parties with a majority in parliament, however, which forces parties to cooperate to form governments that may or may not have a majority behind them. Proportional elections also strengthen internal party cohesion because candidates are dependent on party votes. Understanding the political parties is vital to understanding the Nordics' consensual politics.

The Nordic countries have had proportional electoral systems since the first quarter of the twentieth century. This system means that the distribution of seats in a Nordic parliament is quite close to the distribution of votes among the political parties at a general election. This is unlike a first-past-the-post system, where the distribution of seats may deviate significantly from the election results. In Denmark, a party must have at least 2 percent of the votes to be represented in parliament, whereas the threshold in Norway and Sweden is 4 percent, and in Iceland 5 percent, while Finland does not have a threshold.

Voters, the basis of any democracy, differ in interests and political involvement. The Scandinavian electorates are known to be comparatively interested in politics (European Social Surveys 2021). They have a high level of trust in other people in general, and also in their democracies and national democratic institutions (Svendsen 2021; Andersen & Dinesen 2018). They also value their democratic institutions highly (European Social Survey 2014).

The Scandinavian electorate is politically active in general elections with high turnouts, as shown in Table 6.1. Other countries, such as the Netherlands and Germany, also have high election turnouts.

Party systems

Political parties are the key actors in the decision-making systems of the Nordic parliaments. The Scandinavian party systems share several traits, but have diversified somewhat over the years. The old Scandinavian parties arose based on important societal or class groupings and social movements (Hansen & Kosiara-Pedersen 2017). The dominant cleavages in the population were urban-rural and employer-employee. Norway, Finland,

Table 6.1 Voter turnout at national elections in selected countries, 2012-2022

	Elections 2012-2015	Elections 2017-2019	Latest election
Denmark	85.9 (2015)	84.6 (2019)	84. 1 (2022)
Norway	77.7 (2013)	78.2 (2017)	77.2 (2021)
Sweden	83.3 (2014)	87.2 (2018)	84.1 (2022)
Finland	70.1 (2015)	72.8 (2019)	72.8 (2019)
UK	65.1 (2015)	68.8 (2017)	67.3 (2019)
Germany	71.5 (2013)	76.2 (2017)	76.6 (2021)
The Netherlands	74.6 (2012)	81.9 (2017)	78.1 (2021)
France, parliament, 2nd round	55.4 (2012)	42.6 (2017)	46.2 (2022)

Source: Voter Turnout Database. //www.idea.int/data-tools/data/voter-turnout-database

and Sweden also, because of their size, had pronounced center-periphery cleavage. The Scandinavian countries all have strong *social-democratic parties*, although with some differences. Sweden had the strongest social-democratic party, which governed uninterrupted from 1932 to 1976 – a record never surpassed in any democratic country for a single political party. Both Norway and Sweden have also had social-democratic one-party majority governments.

All of the large Nordic countries have center-right *agrarian parties* (called "center parties" in Norway, Sweden, and Finland; the fiscal-liberal party *Venstre* in Denmark also falls into this category), reflecting the strength of agriculture and fisheries. They have survived the drastic reduction in the number of people employed in these sectors and gained a foothold in the towns and cities, with some success. *Conservative parties*, with their urban and petit bourgeois voters, and *social-liberal parties*, with a share of urban white-collar voters and less affluent rural voters, also belong among the old parties.

While these four types of parties have their roots in the late nineteenth and early twentieth century, several parties have been established since, most disappearing after some years. However, two types have entered the Scandinavian party systems, apparently to stay. One is *socialist parties*, which lie to the left of the social-democratic parties. Denmark has two of these (the Red-Green Alliance and the Socialist Peoples' Party), and so does Norway (the Socialist Left Party and Red), while Sweden has one (the Left Party). Contrary to the communist parties, which had close links to the Soviet Union and disappeared or were reformed with the fall of the Soviet regime, at least as parliamentary parties, the present socialist parties all accept the legitimacy of parliamentary democracy.

The other apparently permanent new party type is *anti-immigrant parties*, positioned to the right on immigration and law and order, but typically closer to the political center-left on redistribution and economic policy (Jungar 2017). In Denmark and Norway, such parties (called the Progress Party in both countries) began by protesting against *big government* and the *system* in the 1970s, when both countries had few immigrants. As immigration increased, these parties turned to restrictive immigrant policy platforms (most notably in Denmark, which saw the birth of the Danish People's Party, causing the death of the Progress Party) and attracted many voters. In Sweden, the anti-immigrant party (called the Sweden Democrats) began as a protest against liberal immigration laws. Initially, the Sweden Democrats as a party were much further to the right than their Danish and Norwegian counterparts, but have now come to resemble them more. This party was something of a political pariah in Sweden until 2022, when it became a supporting party for a center-right minority government that had a much more restrictive anti-immigrant policy than previous governments.

The rise of political issues that are not rooted in the industrial society – such as immigration, and law and order – has added yet another political dimension to the traditional left-right dichotomy in Scandinavian politics. This new dimension has been given different names, such as authoritarianism versus anti-authoritarianism, or just *new politics*. The Danish People's Party, established in 1995, has a strong anti-immigration and law and order platform, but actually its positions on income redistribution and social policy are much closer to the political center-left (Kosiara-Pedersen 2020). This made the party attractive to many traditional Social Democratic voters who shared its anti-immigrant position. Prior to the 2019 election in Denmark, the Social Democrats adopted a more restrictive immigration policy, with success. Enough voters returned to enable the Social Democrats to form a single-party minority government in 2019 (Nedergaard 2022). In the 2019 election, yet another anti-immigration party, which had far more liberal economic policy goals – *Nye Borgerlige*, the "new right" – entered the Danish parliament, and in the 2022 general election, the Danish People's Party ended up as the smaller of the two.

The Scandinavian electorates are generally concerned with environmental and climate policy, yet the party systems in these three countries do not have very strong *green parties*. The Green Party in Sweden has had some success with parliamentary representation; the analogous Norwegian party little success; and the Danish environmental parties no success at all. The traditional parties, particularly the social-democratic parties, were quick to make environmental policy an integrated part of their political platforms. In all three countries it was particularly the socialist parties, left of the social-democratic parties, that built relatively strong environmental platforms from the early 1970s onwards, preventing any strong green parties from rising to prominence. Indeed, the official name of Denmark's most left-leaning political party is the Red-Green Alliance (Seeberg & Kölln 2020), which is, in fact, an alliance of small left-wing parties, including the former pro-Soviet communist party.

The Scandinavian party systems have been characterized as "open, yet stable" (Green-Pedersen & Kosiara-Pedersen 2020) in the sense that the four old types still play a major role in Scandinavian politics, while the systems are open to new arrivals. Most of these new parties are short-lived, but some do gain a more permanent foothold. The balance between stability and openness has protected the party systems from the breakdowns seen in other countries, such as France and Italy, and the Nordic countries still subscribe to a consensual approach in politics.

Despite the dimensions added to the party systems and the fragmentation caused by new parties, the blocs around the old left-right dimension are key to understanding how cooperations and coalitions are formed in the Nordic region. Each country has a center-right bloc and a center-left bloc. The bloc allegiances of each party are well known, and it is rare to see an established party switch bloc. In Denmark, for instance, the Social Liberal Party is the only party that shifts its position between the center-right and center-left blocs, but since 1993 it has been part of the center-left bloc (Green-Pedersen & Skjæveland 2020). The Danish general election in 2022 ended in a majority government (consisting of the Social Democrats, *Venstre*, and the Moderates) which was not bloc-based. It is still too early to say whether this government heralds a new turn in Danish politics, but it is worth noting that the traditional economic left-right dimension defines the blocs in Denmark, not the *new politics* dimension. The next section on minority governments will explain why bloc politics is so important in Scandinavia.

Party discipline is very high among Scandinavian parties with parliamentary seats, unlike situations often seen in the UK and the US. This is a precondition for running efficient minority governments, whether single-party or coalition. Between 2007 and 2018 the Danish parliament passed 2,320 laws. For 2.7 percent of them, one or more MPs deviated from their party line during the final vote. In other words, 97.3 percent of all laws that were passed were passed by MPs voting in accordance with their party line. These figures cover some variation over time: In the parliamentary year 2016/17, no bill was passed in parliament with any MPs deviating from the party vote, compared to 7.2 percent bills in 2011/12 passed with at least one MP deviating from the party line (Green-Pedersen & Skjæveland 2020). The many deviations in the latter example were due to controversies in the Social Democratic-led minority coalition government. Party discipline is not at the same level across all policy areas. And particularly on moral issues, party groups often give MPs freedom to vote according to their convictions.

Minority governments

The Scandinavian countries apply slightly different versions of parliamentarism. Denmark and Norway rely on a principle of *negative parliamentarism*, meaning that a new government can be formed if there is not a majority against it. Sweden relies, in principle, on a system of *positive parliamentarism*, meaning that a new government must carry an investiture vote in parliament. However, since the 1970s the interpretation of this principle has been that a new Swedish government cannot have an absolute majority against it (Hansen 2017). This interpretation puts Sweden closer to being a negative parliamentary system than one that requires an explicit majority in favor of a new government. In practice, then, the three Scandinavian countries are close to applying similar – negative – parliamentary principles.

While some might think the difference between positive and negative parliamentarism is mainly a point of academic interest, it has a major impact on the ease and speed with which governments can be formed. This is because negative parliamentarism does not presuppose that a government's supporting parties will endorse the new government. Negative parliamentarism thus also promotes minority governments (Strøm 1990). It promotes consensual politics because parties in government tend to find solutions as they move to pursue their agendas.

Most Scandinavian governments are minority governments, but with significant differences among the three countries. Denmark has had only four majority governments since adopting its 1953 constitution (1957-1960, 1968-1971, 1993-1994, and 2022-), and is said to hold a world record in minority governments after World War II. Norway has had seven majority governments out of 25 governments since World War II. Measured in years, Norway has had minority governments 44 percent of the time since 1945 (Rommetvedt 2017). Sweden has relied on more single-party minority and majority governments – all but one of them Social Democratic – than the other two countries, and 64 percent of Swedish governments between 1945 and 2015 have been minority governments (Wockelberg 2015). This is also true for its post-2015 governments.

Before a coalition government is installed – be it a minority or majority government – its parties prepare a program listing the policy goals the new government intends to pursue. The extent to which a government can realize its program depends partly on its parliamentary strength, since it is easier to pursue a common goal for a majority government than for a minority government (Christiansen & Pedersen 2014). Supporting parties that are not part of the government can make prior agreements with the government that vary in scope.

According to conventional wisdom, minority governments should produce several deficiencies, the most significant of which are instability, a lack of governability, and poor economic management. Danes living in the early 1980s were probably easy to convince of this wisdom. What soon after became known as the "earthquake election" in 1973[10] came close to breaking down the old party system: The number of parties in parliament doubled, and the four old parties suffered severely. The new protest parties were not fit to take on government responsibilities, however. When the oil crises of the 1970s hit the Western world, along with industrial restructuring, it was particularly challenging for shifting Danish governments to set and follow a reasonable course.

10. The Danish general election in 1973 – later referred to by the Danish word *jordskred*, literally "landslide" – was not one party's victory, but a shifting of the whole political landscape, as the four old parties (Social Democrats, Conservatives, fiscal-liberals, and social-liberals) lost more than a third of their voters, some to new protest parties and some to smaller, older parties

Denmark held national elections in 1971, 1973, 1975, 1977, 1979, and 1981, meaning twice as often as the normal four-year election period would prescribe. Almost every conceivable economic misfortune beset the Danish economy during this time: low growth, high inflation, balance of payments deficits, public finance deficits, unemployment. In 1979, one social-democratic finance minister left his position with the words: "Some say that we're driving on the edge of the economic abyss. We're not, but we can see it." In 1982, a new conservative-fiscal-liberal government came to power and succeeded in turning the economy in a more balanced direction (Nannestad & Green-Pedersen 2008). During the 1980s, Danish parliamentarians learned not only how to survive, but also how to govern in a responsible way that promoted stability and prosperity.

This brings us to the core of the matter: How can minority governments go hand in hand with responsible policies and outcomes that respond to voter preferences? (See also Strøm 1990).

The first part of the answer to this question lies in the phenomenon of bloc politics, which structures otherwise chaotic political competition. One of the two blocs will have a majority, often a very narrow majority, and the prime minister will normally be the leader of the largest party in the majority bloc. The parties behind the majority bloc will always stand behind their bloc in normal times, in the sense that if the minority bloc suggests a vote of no confidence against the bloc in power, the governing bloc's majority will support the government (Green-Pedersen & Skjæveland 2020). Obviously, the supporting parties behind a minority government risk a new election if they do not support the government in such a situation. Again using Denmark as an example, since the adoption of the 1953 constitution only one government has lost a vote of confidence: a single-party minority government run by *Venstre*, which had only 22 of the Folketing's 179 seats. In normal times, however, bloc politics guarantees governmental stability (Green-Pedersen & Thomsen 2005). At present, the fate of the Danish three-party majority government formed after the general election in 2022 – the first Danish coalition government not based on one of the two blocs, but with the new color combination red-purple-blue – remains to be seen.

Despite these mechanisms, bloc politics does not ensure that all a government's bills will be passed with bloc support. On the contrary: Danish governments often enter political settlements (also discussed below) with parties outside their bloc, even in cases where the government's supporting parties are not part of the coalition. One example is immigration policy: Typically, in a Social Democratic-led minority government the parties left of the social-democratic party are more liberal and lenient than the government, so the government will seek its majority among the center-right parties. In some policy areas there is a tradition of broad coalitions in parliament, for example defense, and legislation on police matters. The government may relent on some preferences, but by forging a broad political settlement, for instance on defense, it will increase the likelihood of it being included in defense agreements in the future, at which time power may lie with the other bloc. Many settlements last three or four years. In processes like these the government may lose policy preferences, but it may also gain future influence by working in broad coalitions. Conversely, in areas where a government has strong policy preferences, it may utilize a narrow majority to propel these preferences to the fore.

Why do opposition parties help keep a government in office? The answer is simple: If a government has a parliamentary majority until the next general election, supporting government-led coalitions and political settlements may be an opposition party's only chance to realize some of its policy preferences.

Table 6.2 shows voting patterns from the final readings of bills in the Danish parliament over a period of 45 years. In many periods, the Folketing passed more than 50 percent of bills with a broader majority than needed. Notably, under the minority coalition government of 1978-1979, which consisted of the Social Democrats and the fiscal-liberal party in 1978-1979, a remarkable 88 percent of all bills were passed with a broad majority. The lowest share, 39 percent of bills carried by a broad majority, was seen both in 1993-1994 (under a majority government led by Social Democrats) and in 2007-2011 (under a fiscal-liberal-conservative minority government). The share of bills passed on bloc votes alone has never exceeded 20 percent in the twenty-first century.

Table 6.2 Voting patterns on bills passed in the Danish parliament, 1973-2018

Year/government	**Unanimous**	**Bloc majority**	**Broad majority**	**Total/N**
		Percent		
1973-1975, center-right	32	8	60	100/118
1975-1977, social-democratic	24	1	76	100/399
1977-1978, social-democratic	20	2	78	100/290
1978-1979, broad coalition	12	0	88	100/156
1979-1981, social-democratic	17	2	81	100/325
1981-1982, social-democratic	16	23	62	100/159
1982-1984, center-right	25	20	56	100/173
1984-1987, center-right	23	20	57	100/651
1987-1988, center-right	23	0	77	100/93
1988-1990, center-right	30	18	51	100/415
1990-1993, center-right	44	7	49	100/491
1993-1994, social-democratic	36	25	39	100/399
1994-1998, social-democratic	34	16	50	100/780
1998-2001, social-democratic	30	16	54	100/778
2001-2005, center-right	33	19	47	100/678
2005-2007, center-right	38	14	48	100/584
2007-2011, center-right	45	15	39	100/819
2011-2015, social-democratic	40	10	51	100/735
2015-2018, center-right	42	7	51	100/649

Source: Green-Pedersen & Skjæveland (2020)

The Danish finance act, which is processed and re-adopted each year, is a showcase of consensual politics. The government proposes its finance bill for the coming years in late August, and a settlement is usually reached in the latter half of November. Only a few percent of the total budget is really up for negotiation, but considerable efforts are invested in negotiating small parts of it. These negotiations give the parties a good opportunity to promote their preferred solutions to all kinds of problems. The finance bill negotiations are also a good forum for striking bargains, because parties can give and take, insisting and conceding on different points where their preferences differ, as long as they can find a majority. The final bill may include 20 to 25 compromise agreements on a wide range of issues.

When the time comes to vote on adopting the finance bill, the Folketing first votes for all the different agreements approved by different majorities. In the final vote, all "responsible" parties vote in favor, even the "responsible" opposition parties. This process respects the principle that in order to rule, a government needs funding for its projects. The so-called *responsible* parties are typically those prepared to enter a government coalition, should the possibility arise. The Danish finance act for the fiscal year 2022 was adopted by a very large majority. Only two small center-right parties and one small left-wing party voted against it.

The art of the political settlement

With such thoroughgoing coalitions there must be some norms governing the behavior of the political parties. Shifting Danish governments have developed the art of reaching political settlements (Pedersen 2011; Christiansen & Pedersen 2014; Green-Pedersen & Skjæveland 2020), which are written agreements about a piece of legislation or a major reform. Such a settlement is more than just an agreement about the contents of a bill or a reform, since it impacts on a party's ability to influence future settlements; while it is politically binding, however, it is not a legally binding document.

Political settlements have a long history in the Folketing (Pedersen 2011). During the first three to four decades after World War II, the political parties typically signed a couple of settlements every year, in some years even a handful. Such documents could address defense issues, developing the police force, old-age pensions, or housing regulations; no politically relevant decision is too large or too small to be the object of a political settlement. During the 1990s the number of settlements reached each year rose considerably, and in the 2010s the number was quite impressive.

Political settlements are informal. One political party cannot take another to court to argue that they are not complying. However, defecting from such a settlement comes at a political price, and credibility is a highly esteemed political quality. The following norms apply to political settlements: Changes require the consent of all participating parties, so each party can veto a change. New parties may be allowed on board, provided that all parties already participating agree. (This condition is suspended when a party enters a coalition government, however, because the coalition partners automatically inherit the settlements such a party has signed.) A party can leave a political settlement by announcing its intention to do so before an election. This frees the party from its obligations under the settlement after the election. Some settlements have a sunset clause, while others run until they are terminated by one or more parties.

Political settlements are an important means of governability in systems typified by minority governments. They help overcome potential problems related to minority governments, such as the lack of capacity to address important problems, a lack of economic responsibility, and instability. However, they also come at a price. First, the principle of governmental transparency is violated. In Denmark there is no transparency requirement for agreements or negotiations between political parties, as such negotiations are not an integral part of the state administration. Another problem is that, paradoxically, political settlements may be an obstacle to flexibility. In a country that may have over a hundred settlements in force at any given time, governments may, and sometimes do, end up in a predicament, unable to reach an agreement on some issue because one or more involved parties has obligations under existing settlements that contradict the new settlement, in whole or in part. In most cases a solution is found through a super-majority – which, as mentioned, has more participating parties than strictly necessary to achieve a majority. This way the party that is in a pinch can be kept out of all, or part of, a political settlement.

To sum up, the Scandinavian tradition of consensual politics also characterizes the political life in parliament. The electoral system, with its low threshold for seats and many political parties, made majority governments difficult to form, but enhanced the need for parties to cooperate. Over time such cooperation became stabilized and was in effect informally institutionalized as a prevailing norm for reaching political settlements and building alliances. Consensual politics has also become a norm preferred by many voters in the region, who like broad coalitions and the predictability and stability they produce. Nevertheless, some political decisions are highly controversial and are passed into law by a slender majority, which is sometimes the smallest possible majority.

Chapter 7.

Reforming between consensus and conflict

Political history has countless examples of failed reforms. Reform ideas that never entered the decision-making arena; reform ideas that expired at their birth; reforms that were decided but never implemented; and implemented reforms that missed their mark. The road to successful reforms is paved with stumbling blocks, in the Nordic countries as elsewhere. Nevertheless, reforms do happen. The Nordic parliamentary governance systems have few or no checks and balances – unlike, for instance, the system in the US. If a government controls a majority or can create one, the road is open for reform. In theory, parliamentary majorities are constrained only by the constitution and their own imagination. In the real world, however, governments also calculate voter reactions to reforms, and they must maneuver carefully to earn the consent of, or avoid resistance from, interest groups with the capacity to support or mobilize against reform (Christiansen, Nørgaard, & Sidenius 2004).

Stakeholders are therefore important reform players. If reformers can leave powerful stakeholders better off after a reform, their likelihood of success is higher, compared to a situation in which one or more powerful stakeholders ends up suffering a loss. In rough terms, the reforms that built the Nordic countries during the nineteenth century did the former, whereas more contemporary reforms have done the latter (Öberg et al. 2011).

As shown in previous chapters, the Nordic countries were quite successful in developing their societies from the late eighteenth century over the next hundred years, balancing different societal interests in a mostly peaceful, or at least consensual, way. Labor market institutions averted conflicts between employers and employees. Compromises were reached on benefit programs that prevented the unemployed, ill, disabled, and elderly from living in poverty and misery. The establishment of systems for universal healthcare and education, childcare, and eldercare was not conflict free, but these projects were eventually seen through with the consent of major stakeholders in society. The costs were mostly borne by taxpayers, so the Nordic countries were and are high-tax countries, although the extent of this difference from the many other European countries with lower taxes has diminished. In that sense, high taxes may be a corollary of consensual politics.

Today there is a general consensus among the political and business elites that tax levels in the Nordics should not be significantly raised. Reforms must be financed within the existing tax level. More often than before, reforms imply one or more losing stakeholders, and in a consensual setting it is difficult to convince losers to endorse reforms that will not benefit them. Consequently, consensual policy-making implies linear policy changes that stay within the acceptance zones of the involved stakeholders (Christiansen 2020). In most cases this is also true of both small and large policy reforms in the Nordic region. The politics of forming a program and reforming a program can be very different (Pierson 1996).

What happens if policy entrepreneurs insist on reforms that are outside the acceptance zone of powerful actors? Are such reforms feasible? This is explored in the next two sections: first in terms of the reform of the local and regional government systems in Denmark and Norway, and second through controversial labor market reforms in Denmark. A third section then looks at creating sustainable pension systems in Denmark and Sweden, an increasingly pertinent issue in many countries.

Regional government reforms

The Danish general election in 2001 led to the formation of a minority government consisting of the fiscal-liberals of *Venstre* and the Conservatives, to which the Danish People's Party had pledged its permanent support. Together, these three parties held a parliamentary majority. Local and regional government reform was not initially a high priority for the new government, but in the fall of 2002 an inquiry commission was set up to analyze the pros and cons of the existing local and regional government structure. A reform of the structure in the capital area around Copenhagen had been tested, but it was abandoned in the mid-1990s, based on the findings of a commission report. The members of the new 2002 local government commission were key civil servants at national level, municipal and county representatives, and some experts. The commission, whose white paper was released in January 2004, discussed amalgamating municipalities and merging counties, and redistributing tasks among the different tiers of government, but it did not make specific recommendations (Christiansen & Klitgaard 2009).

The government did not signal any preferences when it received the white paper, but it invited stakeholders to respond in an unusually long consultation process and a broad debate, which ran until April 1, 2004. January through April that year was a busy time for the Danish minister of the interior. As the many issues were discussed publicly across the country, the minister forged a political majority in favor of a rather radical proposal to close down Denmark's 14 counties and set up five new regions instead. Although many people, including county representatives, had expected to see fewer counties (streamlining the public hospitals, which were run by the counties), hardly anyone had expected to see a proposal stripping the new regions of all county tasks, except that of running the hospitals. This was the most controversial part of the reform, which also radically reduced the number of municipalities. The government's proposal was released on April 27, 2004. In line with the Danish tradition when molding major reform packages, the minister tried to create a broad coalition in favor of the reform. At least the Social Democrats would normally be part of such a large reform, but the government was never able to rally support for a broad political settlement. Instead, on June 24, 2004 a narrow majority signed an accord on the largest administrative reform ever decided in Denmark (Christiansen & Klitgaard 2009).

The Danish local government reform was indeed impressive in terms of its size and range. However, it was not consensual. The reform contradicted the principle of consulting the affected interests and stakeholders. The political process contradicted the corporatist tradition, according to which privileged interest groups are invited into the engine room of important political decisions. The Danish association of counties was neither invited in for negotiations nor consulted, because the counties were believed – as was, in fact, the case – to oppose the reform's plans to reduce the tasks of the new regions. In contrast, the organization of the municipal authorities, Local Government Denmark (LGD), was an integrated part of the negotiations throughout the spring of 2004. LGD was offered new tasks mainly related to labor market administration. Some later referred to this situation as fratricide.

As noted, the reform never gained any broad parliamentary consensus. Local and regional government issues were traditionally embraced by consensus from the two largest local and regional government parties, the Social Democrats and the fiscal-liberals. Not so this time. The government invited the Social Democrats for negotiations and gave some concessions, but not enough for the party to support the reform. The large legal complex, 49 bills all told, were adopted in parliament during the summer of 2005. Some of these bills were passed with a supermajority of votes, but the main bills – those establishing the architecture behind the Danish local and regional governance structure – were only adopted by a narrow coalition.

It later came to light that the minister had used several strategies to neutralize reform opponents (Blom-Hansen et al. 2011). He caused confusion by controlling and manipulating information; the government revealed its true preferences late in the process; and the minister used a divide-and-rule strategy by making an alliance with LGD and keeping the Danish association of counties in the dark. Finally, he "bribed" LGD to support the reform by offering the municipal governments new tasks, including labor market administration, in exchange for their support. The reform reduced the number of municipalities in Denmark from 271 to 98. Drawing on these strategic and tactical instruments, the minister succeeded in enacting a major reform within a relatively short time frame.

The 2005 general election in Norway resulted in a majority coalition government consisting of three parties: the Labour Party (Social Democrats), the Socialist Left Party, and the Centre Party. Shortly after the election the government announced that it would pursue a reform at the regional level before 2010 (Fimreite & Selle 2009). Being a majority government should make a reform easy, at least at a parliamentary level, even if this specific reform was primarily a proposal promoted by the Centre Party.

The government released a white paper in 2006, according to which an undecided number of regional-level elected bodies would replace Norway's existing 19 counties by 2010. The new regions would be responsible for regional development and innovation, for the previously central-government offices for agriculture, natural resources, and highway maintenance, and also for most of the tasks the old counties had handled: secondary education, transport, and cultural heritage. The exact number of regions would be announced in a new white paper in spring 2008 (Blom-Hansen et al. 2012).

Up to this point, the reform processes in the two countries were fairly similar, but they later took different paths. After the consultation round following the new Norwegian white paper in early 2008, the government first signaled a preference for 12–15 new regions, only to declare by the end of 2008 that the reform had been abandoned. While the Danish reform was promoted by the control of information, divide and rule, and compensating one stakeholder at the cost of others, the Norwegian decision-making process was open. Furthermore, it did not exploit potential conflicts between municipalities and counties – which would have been difficult because the Norwegian Association of Local and Regional Government, as the name indicates, organizes both levels – and there was no attempt to compensate one stakeholder at the cost of others. Nor is there evidence of the Norwegian government trying to compensate certain actors in order to win their support for the reform (Blom-Hansen et al. 2012). The process was halted for some time. Not until 2020 was the regional reform in Norway finalized, with 11 new regions assigned tasks that were close to those proposed in the 2006 white paper.

The two cases show very similar countries trying to reform their political-administrative structure in very similar ways, but with very different outcomes: Denmark with a reform process that was rapid and efficient (the latter in the sense of the government getting what it wants), and Norway with a slow reform that failed in the short term, but was realized 15 years later. These cases illustrate potential dilemmas between reform efficiency and consensual politics. The Danish process was everything but consensual, yet efficient. The Norwegian process was consensual but less efficient, at least in the short term.

Labor market reforms in Denmark

The reform of the political-administrative structure is not the only case of non-consensual politics in Denmark. Flexible use of the labor force, generous unemployment benefits, and an active labor market policy are key to the Nordic labor market model, as shown in Chapter 5. With strong trade unions and strong employer organizations, labor market policy represents weighty vested interests. Employers are interested in flexibility and the availability of labor, among other things, while the trade unions are interested in protecting the labor force, among other things, not least through unemployment benefits and retirement conditions. The social partners (employees and employers) have a common interest in being privileged partners in policy-making processes, which they were during the formation of the Nordic labor market models for most of the twentieth century. They did not always agree with political decisions, but gains and losses were, by and large, evenly distributed between them. If such a consensual decision-making framework is to endure, new decisions must stick to this balance. But what if they don't?

Twenty-five years of Danish labor market reforms, beginning in the mid-1980s, reveal significant breaks with traditional corporatist policy-making. We will follow two tracks as we investigate this period: one on the size and duration of, and eligibility for, unemployment benefits; the other on the makings of an early retirement program.

As for the first track, in the early 1980s the Danish economy had accumulated a large number of structural problems, as already touched upon in earlier chapters. Unemployment was high and the unemployment benefits very generous. Unemployed workers were entitled to benefits for no less than seven years, and the conditions for earning eligibility for a new period were lenient. The Ministry of Finance called the system a "benefit generator" (Christiansen, Nørgaard, & Sidenius 2004: 64). During the 1980s the center-right government imposed rigorous, cost-containing cuts on unemployment benefits by reducing their indexation and lowering benefits for the long-term unemployed. These were simple but controversial reforms, implemented without involving the social partners and under loud protests from the trade unions. A political majority was ready to use its authority to carry out reforms that were controversial but perceived as necessary.

The Danish labor market reforms of the 1990s were less controversial, but still not fully consensual. A center-left government led by the Social Democrats pursued three rounds of labor market reforms relating to the eligibility of recipients, qualifying rules, duration, and lower benefits for young people. The unemployment benefit period was reduced to four years, and a new period could be earned after one year of normal employment. All these elements were controversial and strongly opposed by the trade unions, which, on the other hand, were less opposed to the active policy elements such as greater focus on education and early interventions for young jobless people (Klitgaard & Nørgaard 2014). The trade unions and employer organizations were consulted throughout the processes, but they were also kept at arm's length at certain times along the way, at least compared to traditional practices under social-democratic governments (Christiansen, Nørgaard, & Sidenius 2004).

If the unions regarded the reforms of the 1990s as tough, they must have seen 2010 as a nightmare scenario. In May 2010 the Danish economy was still burdened by the financial crises that had begun in 2008, and the fiscal-liberal-conservative minority government was looking for cuts in government spending as part of its crisis intervention. Its supporting party, the Danish People's Party, suggested cutting unemployment benefits. Within a few days the government – now with a majority to back it up – decided to cut the period of unemployment benefits from four to two years and to double the period for regaining eligibility from one to two years. The unions were not consulted, and were not even aware that the decision was underway (Christiansen 2020). Such decisions are the lifeblood of the trade unions, but despite their forceful protests the government did not waver.

The second track, on labor market reform, relates to an early retirement program introduced in 1979 by a social-democratic-fiscal-liberal government. Under this program people could retire at the age of 60, contingent on at least five years' membership of an unemployment fund. This program was intended for people who were worn down by physically taxing jobs. Estimates from 1979 predicted that 17,000 people would benefit from the program in the future. In 1990, almost 100,000 people received pensions under this program; in 2004 the number peaked at nearly 180,000. It soon became clear to decision-makers that the program was attracting many more people than first estimated, including teachers and nurses. The program was draining the Danish labor market even as aging was becoming a hot topic on the political agenda.

In 1998, a Social Democratic-led government became very unpopular with the trade unions when it made an accord with the fiscal-liberals on cuts to the public early retirement program without informing the social partners. This political settlement implied lower compensation rates, later entry into the program, and partial co-funding by future recipients. In addition, the accord lowered the general retirement age from 67 to 65 years (Kristiansen & Ræbild 2001). Although the reform reduced the value of the early retirement, the program was still popular among employees getting close to retirement age. The center-right governments in power from 2001 through 2011 hesitated to cut the program further, due to the reactions they had seen back in 1998. However, in the aftermath of the financial crisis, in 2011 the government did propose further cuts, again doing so without negotiating with the social partners (Elmelund-Præstekær, Klitgaard, & Schumacher 2015). Today's eligibility criteria for the early retirement program and its coverage limit its appeal.

These two examples show that since the 1980s the Danish Trade Union Federation, or FH, has lost power in relation to labor market decision-making. Politicians did not believe FH would be able to deliver in the political give and take on issues like cuts to unemployment benefits and the early retirement program. That does not mean, however, that FH lost all its clout. During the 1980s and the 2000s when these cuts were on the agenda, FH was acting as a traditional partner in other decisions. Mailand (2011) lists eight tripartite agreements made on labor market issues between 1980 and 2011, six of which were carried through under center-right governments. Consensual, co-operative relations were upheld in certain parts of labor market policy-making, while other parts were conflictual.

Pension reforms in Denmark and Sweden

Retirement pension systems are an important part of Nordic welfare thinking. They secure an income for people after their work lives are over, and as such are long-term contracts between citizens and pension sponsors. Depending on how they are put together, pension systems also affect the national economy, labor market participation, retirement age, taxes, income equality, and health, just to mention their most important areas of impact.

Aging populations in most Western countries confront decision-makers with multiple problems for the future economic sustainability of their systems. Pressing issues include retirement age, pension financing, increasing demands for healthcare, and nursing capacity. In the following section we will look only at the financial aspect: how pensions are financed.

Pensions, sometimes called *retirement benefits*, can be financed with money that is simultaneously collected and paid out to pensioners. This model, called a *pay-as-you-go* (PAYGO) system, can be financed by tax or based on labor market contributions. The other model, called a *funded pension system*, accumulates dedicated assets to cover the pension plan's liabilities to pensioners (OECD Pensions Outlook 2022).

With aging populations it is preferable to run a funded pension system for the simple reason that with this model, the money for current pensioners will be there without burdening today's taxpayers. So why not introduce a funded system in all countries? First, this is easier said than done. Moving from a PAYGO system to a funded system means that the current sponsors have to pay not only for current pensioners, but also for the pensioners of the future. The only way to move from one system to the other would be stepwise, over a very long period of time, in order to relieve the burden on current sponsors. Moving the other way, from a funded system to a PAYGO system, would meet the reverse problem, in that current pensioners would receive a PAYGO pension as well as a funded pension (Green-Pedersen & Lindbom 2006).

Over the last 30 to 40 years, Denmark and Sweden have followed different paths in developing their pension systems. Denmark has a primarily funded system, while Sweden primarily relies on a PAYGO system with some funding. In 2021, Denmark and Sweden had retirement savings amounting to 230 and 120 percent of their GDP, respectively. Norway is a Nordic outlier with very little retirement savings. Appearances are deceptive, however: The Norwegian state-owned oil fund, often referred to simply as "the pension fund", holds assets corresponding to 250 percent of Norway's GDP (2022). Just one third of OECD countries have substantive earmarked retirement assets (OECD 2022).

Denmark was the second country in the world to introduce a pension system, which it did in 1891. Chancellor Bismarck had introduced a German system in 1889, financed by mandatory contributions from employers and employees, whereas the Danish system, begun two years later, was financed purely by tax and targeted needy citizens aged 60 and over. Many years later, in the late 1950s, Denmark decided to introduce a universal flat-rate pension for all citizens aged 67 and up, also financed by tax. In 1964, another layer was added with the introduction of another flat-rate, rather small "labor-market supplementary pension" called *Arbejdsmarkedets Tillægspension* (ATP), which is based on contributions from employers and employees. In the following years the future of the Danish pension system was on the political agenda several times, spurred by calculations of the future pension burden and by increasing inequality, due to the superior pension plans for public sector civil servants and white-collar employees in the private sector (Andersen & Larsen 2004). Those two groups made it difficult to develop a PAYGO system because of the large sums already invested in funded pensions for them. In 1987, the center-right government entered into a tripartite agreement with top-level negotiators for the social partners, pledging that if funded labor market pensions became part of the regular collective agreements between employers and employees, the Danish state would back the system with the necessary legislation. The 1991 collective agreement negotiated for the private sector stated that 0.9 percent of annual wages and salaries was to be set aside for pensions. After a number of years this was raised to between 10 and 18 percent, depending on one's sector of employment (Kangas, Lundberg, & Ploug 2010).

In the case of Denmark, the funded system was established as a mix of top-down and bottom-up mechanisms by the social partners, facilitated by supportive government regulations. While the process – with pervasive intervention from the social partners – was typically Nordic in style, the Danish system today differs from the Nordic model in that it is a bifurcated system with a universal basic pension for all citizens financed by tax (half of it means-tested and thus dependent on one's total income), as well as a "labor market pension", *Arbejdsmarkeds-pension* (AMP) which is a mandatory company pension based on the 10-18 percent of an employee's wage/salary earnings mentioned earlier, and administered by private pension funds. The Danish pension system is one of the most highly funded systems in the world.

The Swedes took a different path to a partly funded system. While Denmark was very early to introduce a (means-tested) pension system, Sweden was the first country in the world to introduce a universal basic pension in 1913. This was a partly funded and partly means-tested system, but nevertheless with a universal pension for all citizens aged 67 and over (Hagen 2017). A reform in 1935 made the Swedish system less funded and introduced a larger element of means-tested pension. In 1946, the remaining part of the funded system was removed, turning the Swedish system into a purely PAYGO system, while at the same time introducing a new element: a universal flat-rate pension that substantially increased income for the poorest pensioners (Hagen 2013). In 1960, Sweden added a new and politically controversial PAYGO element with its so-called ATP, a "general supplementary pension" based (much like Denmark's ATP from 1964) on earnings-related contributions made by all those active on the labor market. This raised the benefit level again, but it declined in value for the highest-earning groups as the years went on (Hagen 2017; Green-Pedersen & Lindbom 2006). By the early 1990s it had become clear that Sweden needed an extensive pension reform. Contrary to the Danish process, which was mainly bottom-up, the Swedish system was top-down. A parliamentary working group was formed to create a system that was more responsive to the state of the economy, created a clearer link between contributions and benefits, and encouraged long-term saving (Hagen 2017). Employer organizations and trade unions were not involved in the decision-making process. After some years of work, the new Swedish system was adopted in 1998, scheduled to be implemented by 1999. The Swedish system now consists of three tiers: (1) a minimum guarantee for those with no or little earnings-related pension; (2) an earnings-related pension financed by employers and employees, of 16 percent of one's earnings (noting that (1) and (2) are both pay-as-you-go systems); and finally (3) a fully funded earnings-related element of 2.5 percent of one's earnings, allocated to an individual financial account and co-funded by employer and employee (Hagen 2017).

The transformation of the Danish pension system from a PAYGO system to a strongly funded system would not have happened without the strong position of employers and trade unions in the governance of the Danish labor market regime, in which almost all employees are covered by a collective labor market agreement or work under conditions as if they were. The process also reveals a high level of trust and cooperation between the Danish government and social partners – as the social partners had to rely on supportive legislation. This is an example of consensual policy-making crossing the borderline between politics and market dynamics. The Swedish case reveals a high level of consensual top-down reform capacity in a complicated policy area with many pitfalls, and with a substantial influence on most people's lives.

The Nordic countries' reform capacity

Although it is difficult to assess precisely, there is hardly any doubt that the Nordic countries have comparatively high capacities for reform. They do have sectors or isolated pockets that lag behind the rest of society, and also lock-ins in which strong vested interests prevent change and reform. Nevertheless, they tend to meet challenges with policy responses that show a comparatively high level of efficiency. This applies to matters such as societal infrastructure, labor market relations, political institutions, and the organization of the public sector.

Paradoxically, the capacity for reform is both promoted and hampered by the Nordic policy-making style. Consensual policy-making is efficient in promoting reform if all powerful actors get their (fair) share of the pie. This, however, also restricts the direction that reform can take. Reforms that go beyond linear change become difficult, sometimes impossible, if consensual norms are still observed – yet radical reforms do happen, in the Nordic countries as elsewhere. The Danish and Norwegian regional-municipal reforms were both all-encompassing, although in different ways. By deviating from the Nordic policy-making style, the Danish government delivered a radical reform less than three years after the idea was conceived. The Norwegians stuck to consensual policy-making and delivered the reform, but it took considerably longer.

From the mid-1990s through 2010, Danish governments succeeded in making highly controversial labor market decisions by keeping the social partners at arm's length or entirely out of the decision-making process, yet staying within consensual norms in encounters about various other policy issues with the same partners. Consensual policy-making may be broken in one area but respected in another, even with the same actors in both instances. The unions did not defect from the parts of labor market policy where they were still active partners just because they were excluded from other parts. Defection would not have served the interests of their members.

The pension reform examples above show that it is possible to reform core policies in areas of major importance to society, such as pensions, in a cooperative and consensual way. One aim, as in Denmark, can be to delegate the power to form a new pension system to the social partners. The result was a piecemeal transformation of the pension system into one of the most financially founded systems in the world. Alternatively, as in the Swedish system, the aim can be to formulate and implement the reform within a small cross-party parliamentary group.

In short, reforms are indeed possible in the Nordic countries. When consensual policy-making is not feasible, parliamentary majorities may be willing to use their power in a conflictual way.

Chapter 8.

Conclusions

People in the Nordic region live in societies which have developed institutions that encourage individuals and groups to deal with conflicts in nonviolent, often inclusive, and even consensual ways. The Dutch-American political scientist Arend Lijphart (1999) suggested distinguishing between consensual and majoritarian democracies. The former are typified by proportional voting, multi-party systems, close cooperation between the state and selected interest groups, and, consequently, consensual policy-making.

Several European countries qualify as consensual democracies, among them the Nordics – not least the three Scandinavian countries. They share many characteristics with a number of smaller European countries. However, they also have certain more particular traits in common. One is a bureaucracy recruited on merit, which was installed relatively early in the development of the Nordic countries. In addition, small farmers and workers who mobilized from the bottom up brought self-confidence and coherence to the two classes on which the modern industrial society was built. Farmers are still an influential group, despite their declining numbers, and in all of the Scandinavian countries the historically agrarian parties still play an important role. What is more, among other things the mobilization of workers resulted in comparatively very strong trade unions, which are still active and important political players, and are formally or informally affiliated with the social-democratic parties that have played such important roles in the Nordic region.

The political situations created in these countries resulted from trials and errors in dealing with the opportunities and threats arising from the industrial society. Corporatism – the integration of privileged interest groups in making and implementing policy – became an important institution for political decisions that enjoyed broad political support. When, during the 1970s, the demand for economic reorganization became pressing and corporatist politics proved unable to deliver the politically required solutions, the decision-making style became more autonomous in relation to organized interests, although corporatism was never fully abolished. *Privileged pluralism* denotes a structure in which strong interest groups still play a political role, but at a slightly greater distance from central government actors. In this way, the Nordic countries could also successfully pursue controversial reforms at a pace not often seen in other countries. Consensual policy-making does not rule out reforms that challenge vested interests in favor of linear policy changes.

Strong labor market groups in general, and powerful trade unions in particular, created a labor market model in which flexibility is paired with comparatively high levels of security in terms of unemployment compensation. Active labor market policies resulted in relatively low levels of unemployment, and the state undertook a more active role. Solutions in the Nordics are often a result of the development of strong unions, a high level of equality, strong social-democratic parties, generous and universal welfare states, and, generally speaking, political institutions that predispose actors to consensual political decision-making.

This means that interest groups are included in political decisions when relevant, and when they can and will deliver in the give and take of politics; there is close cooperation between the social partners in the labor market; and consensual decision-making is typical in parliaments, with super-majorities passing many bills.

Finally, it is worth noting that consensual politics also characterizes parliamentary behavior in the region. Most Nordic governments are minority coalition governments that have to seek a majority outside the government itself. Due to bloc politics and a preference for broad political accords on many policy areas, most Nordic laws are adopted by super-majorities, meaning majorities larger than are necessary to pass them. Still, this does not mean that bloc politics cannot cause political decisions, and sometimes even controversial reforms, to be adopted by the smallest possible majority.

Francis Fukuyama (2013) coined the phrase "getting to Denmark", which could easily have been constructed with any of the Nordic countries. Fukuyama was referring, on the one hand, to the desirability of Denmark's political institutions, which produced stability, peace, wealth, democracy, and a low level of corruption. On the other hand, he also criticized some international organizations for presupposing that developing countries have the same preconditions for reform, and reform capacity, as Denmark. The point here is that while there may be reason to envy some aspects of the Nordic countries' institutions and their effects, it is not possible to transfer or install these institutions in countries with very different preconditions. Nevertheless, certain elements of Nordic consensual policy-making can travel to other countries, just as, over the years, the Nordic countries have borrowed many of their good ideas from abroad.

Suggestions for further reading

Andersen, D. D. E. (2023a). Impartial Administration and Peaceful Agrarian Reform: The foundations for democracy in Scandinavia. *American Political Science Review*. In press.

Binderkrantz, A. S., Christiansen, P. M., & Pedersen, H. H. (2014). A Privileged Position? The Influence of Business Interests in Government Consultations. *Journal of Public Administration Research and Theory, 24*(4), 879-896.

Esping-Andersen, G. (1990). *Three Worlds of Welfare Capitalism*. Polity Press and Princeton University Press.

Green-Pedersen, C. & Skjæveland, A. (2020). Governments in Action. Consensual Politics and Minority Governments. In Peter Munk Christiansen, Jørgen Elklit, & Peter Nedergaard (Eds.) (2020), *The Oxford Handbook of Danish Politics*. 230-241. Oxford University Press.

Høgedahl, L. (2020). The Danish labour market model: Is the bumblebee still flying? In Peter Munk Christiansen, Jørgen Elklit, & Peter Nedergaard (Eds.) (2020), *The Oxford Handbook of Danish Politics*. 559-576. Oxford University Press.

Knutsen, O. (Ed.) (2017). *The Nordic Models in Political Science*. Fagbokforlaget.

Rothstein, B. (1992). *Den korporativa staten*. Nordstedts.

Scruggs, L. (2002). The Ghent system and union membership in Europe, 1970-1996. *Political Research Quarterly, 55*(2), 275-297.

References

Allern, E. H., Aylott, N. & Christiansen, F. J. (2007). Social Democrats and trade unions in Scandinavia: The decline and persistence of institutional relationships. *European Journal of Political Research, 46*(5), 607-635.

Andersen, D. D. E. (2023a). Impartial Administration and Peaceful Agrarian Reform: The foundations for democracy in Scandinavia. *American Political Science Review*. In press.

Andersen, D. D. E. (2023b). *State Impartiality and the Development of a Political Society of Compromise in Scandinavia*. Aarhus University: Department of Political Science. Unpublished paper.

Andersen, J. G. & Larsen, C. A. (2004). *Magten på borgen. En analyse af beslutningsprocesser i større politiske reformer*. Aarhus University Press.

Andersen, R. F. & Thisted Dinesen, P. (2017). Social capital in the Scandinavian countries. In Peter Nedergaard & Anders Wivel (Eds.), *The Routledge Handbook of Scandinavian Politics*. 161-173. Routledge.

Andersen, T. M. (2021). *Economic Performance in the Nordic World*. Aarhus University Press & The University of Wisconsin Press.

Arnholtz, J. (2022). The embedded flexibility of Nordic labor market models under pressure from EU-induced dualization – The case of posted work in Denmark and Sweden. *Regulation and Governance*. https://doi.org/10.1111/rego.12461

Binderkrantz, A. S. & Christiansen, P. M. (2015). From Classic to Modern Corporatism. Interest Group Representation in Danish Public Committees in 1975 and 2010. *Journal of European Public Policy, 22*(7), 1022-1039.

Binderkrantz, A. S., Christiansen, P. M. & Pedersen, H. H. (2014). A Privileged Position? The Influence of Business

Interests in Government Consultations. *Journal of Public Administration Research and Theory, 24*(4), 879-896.
Binderkrantz, A. S. & Christiansen, P. M. (2023). Sidste chance: interesseorganisationernes indflydelse ved høringer af lovforslag. In Peter Bjerre Mortensen & Søren Serritzlew (Eds.). *I Statskundskabens tjeneste. Festskrift til Jens Blom-Hansen*. 93-103. Politica.
Bjørnskov, C. (2021). *Happiness in the Nordic World*. Aarhus University Press & The University of Wisconsin Press.
Blake, D. J. (1960). Swedish trade unions and the social democratic party: The formative years. *Scandinavian Economic History Review, 8*(1), 19-44.
Blom-Hansen, J., Christiansen, P. M., Fimreite, A., & Selle, P. (2011). Reform Strategies Matter: Explaining the Perplexing Results of Regional Government Reforms in Norway and Denmark. *Local Government Studies, 38*(1), 70-90.
Christiansen, P. M. (Ed.) (1996). *Governing the Environment. Policy, Politics, and Organization in the Nordic Countries.* Nordic Council of Ministers, Nord 1996, 5.
Christiansen, F. J. & Pedersen, H. H. (2014). Minority coalition governance in Denmark. *Party Politics, 20*(6), 940-949.
Christiansen, P. M. & Rommetvedt, H. (1999). From Corporatism to Lobbyism? Parliaments, Executives, and Organized Interest in Denmark and Norway. *Scandinavian Political Studies, 22*(3), 195-220.
Christiansen, P. M. (1999). Det fælles bedste? Interesseorganisationer, folkestyre og korporatisme. In Jørgen Goul Andersen, Peter Munk Christiansen, Torben Beck Jørgensen, Lise Togeby, & Signild Vallgårda (Eds.), *Den demokratiske udfordring*. 247-266. Hans Reitzels Forlag.
Christiansen, P. M. & Klitgaard, M. B. (2009). Behind the Veil of Vagueness: Success and Failure in Institutional Reform. *Journal of Public Policy, 30*(2), 183-200.

Christiansen, P. M. & Nørgaard, A. S. (2003). *Faste forhold – flygtige forbindelser. Stat og interesseorganisationer i Danmark i det 20. århundrede*. Aarhus University Press.

Christiansen, P. M., Nørgaard, A. S. & Sidenius, N. C. (2004). Hvem skriver lovene? *Interesseorganisationer og politiske beslutninger*. Aarhus University Press.

Christiansen, P. M. & Nørgaard, A. S. (2009). Kommissioner i dansk politik efter 1980. In Jørgen Grønnegård Christensen, Poul Erik Mouritzen, & Asbjørn Sonne Nørgaard (Eds.), *De store kommissioner. Vise mænd, smagsdommere eller nyttige idioter*. University of Southern Denmark Press.

Christiansen, P. M., Mach, A. & Varone, F. (2018). How corporatist institutions shape the access of citizen groups to policy makers: Evidence from Denmark and Switzerland. *Journal of European Public Policy, 25*(4), 526-545.

Christiansen, P. M. (2019). Corporatism (and Neo-Corporatism). In Phil Harris, Alberto Bitonti, Craig S. Fleisher, & Anne Skorkjær Binderkrantz (Eds.). *The Palgrave Encyclopedia of Interest Groups, Lobbying and Public Affairs*. Palgrave Macmillan.

Christiansen, P. M. (2020). Corporatism: Exaggerated Death Rumors? In Peter Munk Christiansen, Jørgen Elklit, & Peter Nedergaard (Eds.) (2020), *The Oxford Handbook of Danish Politics*. 160-176. Oxford University Press.

Christiansen, P. M., Nørgaard, A. S., Rommetvedt, H., Svensson, T., Thesen, G. & Öberg, P. (2010). Varieties of democracy: interest groups and corporatist committees in Scandinavian policy making. *Voluntas*, 21, 22-40.

Christiansen, F. J. (2020). From Agrarian and Liberal to Centre-Right Catch-All. In Peter Munk Christiansen, Jørgen Elklit, & Peter Nedergaard (Eds.) (2020), *The Oxford Handbook of Danish Politics*. 296-313. Oxford University Press.

Crepaz, M. (1992). Corporatism in Decline?: An Empirical Analysis of the Impact of Corporatism on Macroeconomic Performance and Industrial Disputes in 18 Industrialized Democracies. *Comparative Political Studies, 25*(2), 139-168.

Dahlström, C. & Lapuente, V. (2017). *Organizing Leviathan. Politicians, bureaucrats, and the making of good government*. Cambridge University Press.

de Tocqueville, A. (2004/1835). *Democracy in America*. Penguin.

Due, J., Madsen, J. S. & Jensen, C. S. (2000). The 'September Compromise': A Strategic Choice by Danish Employers in 1899. *Historical Studies in Industrial relations*, 10, 43-70.

Elmelund-Præstekær, C., Klitgaard, M. B. & Schumacher, G. (2015). What wins public support? Communicating or obfuscating welfare state retrenchment. *European Political Science Review, 7*(3), 427-450.

Esping-Andersen, G. (1990). *Three Worlds of Welfare Capitalism*. Polity Press and Princeton University Press.

European Social Survey (2014). Europeans' Understandings and Evaluations of Democracy: Topline Results from Round 6 of the European Social Survey. ESS Topline Results Series 4. https://www.europeansocialsurvey.org/sites/default/files/2023-06/TL4-Democracy-English.pdf

European Social Survey (2021). European Research Infrastructure (ESS ERIC).

Fimreite, A. & Selle, P. (2009). Norwegian regions – new wine and old bottles? In Paul G. Roness & Harald Sætren (Eds.), *Changes and continuity*. 191-210. Fagbokforlaget.

Fukuyama, F. (2014). *Political Order and Political Decay: From the Industrial Revolution to the Globalization of Democracy*. Farrar, Straus and Giroux.

Green-Pedersen, C. & Thomsen, L. H. (2005). Bloc politics vs. broad cooperation? The functioning of Danish minority parliamentarism. *The Journal of Legislative Studies, 11*(2), 153-169.

Green-Pedersen, C. & Lindbom, A. (2006). Politics within paths: trajectories of Danish and Swedish earnings-related pensions. *Journal of European Public Policy, 16*(3), 245-258.

Green-Pedersen, C. & Skjæveland, A. (2020). Governments in Action. Consensual Politics and Minority Governments. In Peter Munk Christiansen, Jørgen Elklit, & Peter Nedergaard (Eds.) (2020), *The Oxford Handbook of Danish Politics*. 230-241. Oxford University Press.

Green-Pedersen, C. & Kosiara-Pedersen, K. (2020). The Party System: Open yet Stable. In Peter Munk Christiansen, Jørgen Elklit, & Peter Nedergaard (Eds.) (2020), *The Oxford Handbook of Danish Politics*. 213-229. Oxford University Press.

Greve, B., Blomquist, P., Hvinden, B. & van Gerven, M. (2021). Nordic welfare states – still standing or changed by the COVID-19 crisis? *Social Policy & Administration*, 55, 295-311.

Gooderham, P. N., Navrbjerg, S. E., Olsen, K. M. & Steen, C. R. (2015). The labor market regimes of Denmark and Norway – One Nordic model? *Journal of Industrial Relations, 57*(2), 166-186.

Gundelach, P. (1988). *Sociale bevægelser og samfundsændringer*. Politica.

Hansen, M. E. (2017). Cabinets and ministerial turnover in the Scandinavian countries. In Peter Nedergaard & Anders Wivel (Eds.), *The Routledge Handbook of Scandinavian Politics*. 92-102. Routledge.

Hansen, K. M. & Kosiara-Pedersen, K. (2017). Nordic voters and party systems. In Peter Nedergaard & Anders Wivel (Eds.), *The Routledge Handbook of Scandinavian Politics.* 114-123. Routledge.

Hagen, J. (2013). *A History of the Swedish Pension System.* Working Paper 2013: 7. Uppsala Center for Fiscal Studies.

Hagen, J. (2017). Pension Principles in the Swedish pension system. *Scandinavian Economic History Review, 65*(1), 28-51.

Hesstved, S. & Christiansen, P. M. (2022). The politics of policy inquiry commissions: Denmark and Norway, 1971-2017. *West European Politics, 45*(2), 350-454.

Heggebø, K. (2016). Hiring, employment, and health in Scandinavia: the Danish 'flexicurity' model in comparative perspective. *European Societies, 18*(5), 460-486.

Hobolt, S., James T. & Banducci, S. (2013). Clarity of responsibility: How government cohesion conditions performance voting. *European Journal of Political Research, 52*(2), 164-187.

Høgedahl, L. (2020). The Danish labour market model: Is the bumblebee still flying? In Peter Munk Christiansen, Jørgen Elklit, & Peter Nedergaard (Eds.) (2020), *The Oxford Handbook of Danish Politics*. 559-576. Oxford University Press.

Jensen, C. (2021). *Equality in the Nordic World*. Aarhus University Press & The University of Wisconsin Press.

Jensen, P. H. (2017). Danish Flexicurity: Preconditions and future prospects. *Industrial Relations Journal, 48*(3), 218-240.

Johansen, L. N. & Kristensen, O. P. (1982). Corporatist Traits in Denmark 1946-76. In Gerhart Lehmbruch & Philippe Schmitter (Eds.), *Consequences of Corporatist Policy-Making*. 189-218. Sage.

Jungar, A. (2017). Continuity and convergence. Populism in Scandinavia. In Peter Nedergaard & Anders Wivel (Eds.), *The Routledge Handbook of Scandinavian Politics*. 147-160. Routledge.

Kangas, O., Lundberg, U. & Ploug, N. (2010). Three Routes to Pension Reform: Politics and Institutions in Reforming Pensions in Denmark, Finland and Sweden. *Social Policy and Administration, 44*(3), 265-284.

van Kersbergen, K. & Vis, B. (2022). Digitalization as a policy response to social acceleration: Comparing democratic problem solving in Denmark and the Netherlands. *Government Information Quarterly, 39*(3). https://doi.org/10.1016/j.giq.2022.101707

Kjellberg, A. & Nergaard, K. (2022). Union Density in Norway and Sweden: Stability versus decline. *Nordic journal of working life studies*, 12, 51-72.

Klitgaard, M. B. & Nørgaard, A. S. (2014). Structural Stress or Deliberate Decision? How Governments Have Disempowered Unions in Denmark. *European Journal of Political Research, 53*(2), 404-421.

Knutsen, O. (Ed.) (2017). *The Nordic Models in Political Science*. Fagbokforlaget.

Kristiansen, H. S. & Ræbild, J. (2001). *Efterlønsreformen bag facaden*. Columbus.

Koefoed, N. J. (2017). Social Responsibilities in the Protestant North. Denmark and Sweden in Leen van Molle (Ed.), *The Dynamics of Religious Reform in Northern Europe 1780-1920. Charity and Social Welfare*. 251-280. Leuven University Press.

Kosiara-Pedersen, K. (2020). The Danish People's Party: Centre-oriented populists? In Peter Munk Christiansen, Jørgen Elklit, & Peter Nedergaard (Eds.) (2020), *The Oxford Handbook of Danish Politics*. 313-328. Oxford University Press.

Larsson, T. (1993). *Det svenska statsskicket*. Studentlitteratur.

Lewin, L. (1992). *Samhället och de organiserade intressena*. Norstedts.

Lijphart, A. (1999). *Patterns of Democracy. Government Forms and Performance in Thirty-Six Countries*. Yale University Press.

Mailand, M. (2011). *Trepartssamarbejdet gennem tiderne – hvordan, hvornår og hvilke udfordringer?* FAOS. University of Copenhagen.

Martin, C. J. & Swank, D. (2012) *The Political Construction of Business Interests: Coordination, Growth, and Equality*. Cambridge University Press.

Martin, C. J. (2018). Imagine All the People. Literature, Society, and Cross-National Variation in Educational Systems. *World Politics, 70*(3), 398-442.

Nannestad, P. & Green-Pedersen, C. (2008). Keeping the bumblebee flying. Economic policy in the welfare state of Denmark 1973-99. In Erik Albæk, Leslie C. Eliason, Asbjørn Sonne Nørgaard, & Herman M. Schwartz (Eds.), *Crises, miracles, and beyond. Negotiated adaptation of the Danish welfare state*. 33-74. Aarhus University Press.

Nedergaard, P. (2022). Bucking the trend: The extraordinary bounce back of the Danish center-left. In Georg Mentz (Ed.), *The Resistible Corrosion of Europe's Center-Left after 2008*. 170-190. Routledge.

Nørgaard, A. S. (1997). *The Politics of Institutional Control: Corporatism in Danish Occupational Safety and Health Regulation & Unemployment Insurance, 1870-1995*. Politica.

OECD (2022). *OECD Pensions Outlook 2022*.

Olson, M. (1982). *The Rise and Decline of Nations: Economic Growth, Stagflation, and Social Rigidities*. Yale University Press.

Olson, M. (1990). *How Bright are the Northern Lights? Some Questions about Sweden*. Institute of Economic Research.

Pedersen, H. H. (2010). How intra-party power relations affect the coalition behaviour of political parties, *Party Politics, 16*(6), 737-754.

Pedersen, H. H. (2011). Etableringen af politiske forlig som parlamentarisk praksis. *Politic, 43*(1), 48-67.

Pettersson, O. (2015). Rational Politics: Commissions of Inquiry and the Referral System in Sweden. In Jon Pierre (Ed.), *The Oxford Handbook of Swedish Politics*. 650-662. Oxford University Press.

Pierson, P. (1996). The new politics of the welfare state. *World Politics, 48*, 143-179.

Putnam, R. (2010). *The Origin of Political Order. From Prehuman Time to the French Revolution*. Farrah, Straus & Giroux.

Rommetvedt, H. (2017). *Politikkens allmenngjøring. Stortinget, regeringen og de organiserte interessene i et nypluralistisk demokrati*. Fagbokforlaget.

Rothstein, B. (1992). *Den korporativa staten*. Nordstedts.

Schmitter, P. (1989). Corporatism is Dead! Long Live Corporatism! *Government and Opposition, 24*(1), 54-73.

Scruggs, L. (2002). The Ghent system and union membership in Europe, 1970-1996. *Political Research Quarterly, 55*(2), 275-297.

Seeberg, H. B. & Kölln, A. (2020). The Red-Green Alliance: Is it Red or Green? In Peter Munk Christiansen, Jørgen Elklit & Peter Nedergaard (Eds.) (2020), *The Oxford Handbook of Danish Politics*. 329-346. Oxford University Press.

Skjæveland, A. (2005). Dimensionaliteten i Folketinget: Er der en ny politisk dimension? *Politica, 37*(4), 411-422.

Strøm, K. (1990). *Minority Government and Majority Rule*. Cambridge University Press.

Svenson, T. (2015). The Swedish model of industrial relations. In Jon Pierre (Ed.), *The Oxford Handbook of Swedish Politics*. 612-627. Oxford University Press.

Szczepaniak, M. & Szuic-Obloza, A. (2021). Associations Between Job Satisfaction and Employment Protection in Selected European Union Countries. *European Research Studies*. https://www.doi.org/10.35808/ersj/1979

Wängnerud, L. (2012). How Women Gained Suffrage in Sweden: A Weave of Alliances. In Blanca Rodríguez-Ruiz & Ruth Rubio-Marin (Eds.), *The Struggle for Female Suffrage in Europe*. 241-256.

Weber, M. (1919). *Wirtschaft und Gesellschaft*. Berlin.

Widfeldt, A. (2001). The Swedish Center Party. The Poor Relation of the Family. In David Arter (Ed.), *From Farmland to City Square. The Electoral Adaptation of the Nordic Agrarian Parties*. Routledge.

Wockelberg, H. (2015). Weak Investiture Rules and the Emergence of Minority Governments in Sweden. In Bjørn Erik Rasch, Shane Martin & José Antonio Cheibub (Eds.), *Parliaments and Government Formation: Unpacking Investiture Rules*. 233-250. Oxford University Press.

Voter Turnout Database. //www.idea.int/data-tools/data/voter-turnout-database l

Öberg, P., Svensson, T., Christiansen, P. M., Nørgaard, A. S., Rommetvedt, H. & Thesen, G. (2011). Disrupted Exchange and Declining Corporatism: Government Authority and Interest Group Capability in Scandinavia. *Government and Opposition, 46*(3), 365-391.